Journeys Thr

A True Story

Gone in an Instant

Losing My Son. Loving His Killer.

Tammy Horvath

TYH Publications

ISBN: 978-1-7368861-0-6 (Paperback)

ISBN: 978-1-7368861-1-3 (eBook)

ISBN: 978-1-7368861-2-0 (Audiobook)

ISBN: 978-1-7368861-3-7 (Paperback on Publish Drive)

This book is a memoir. Dialogue has been recreated from memory, and I'm aware that people may remember it quite differently. Some names, places, and dates have been altered to protect the privacy of individuals and make the story more enjoyable; however, the details and dialogue are consistent with my memories and events are true. The author and publisher don't guarantee the accuracy of the information in the book. Gone in an Instant reflects my experiences before and after the death of my son. Nothing was written with the intent of hurting any individual or reader. The opinions expressed in this book are my own.

All Scripture quotations, unless otherwise indicated, are taken from the Holy Bible, New International Version®, NIV®. Copyright © 1973, 1978, 1984, 2011 by Biblica, Inc.™ Used by permission of Zondervan. All rights reserved worldwide. www.zondervan.com. The "NIV" and "New International Version" are trademarks registered in the United States Patent and Trademark Office by Biblica, Inc.™

First edition published 2020. Second edition published 2022.

Printed in the United States of America

TYH Publications

117 Forest Street, Sidman, PA 15955

CONTENTS

Dedication   1

1. Gone!   2

2. A Mother's Worst Nightmare   4

3. Dysfunctional   8

4. First Loves   14

5. Love of My Life   20

6. True Colors   25

7. A Marriage Proposal   30

8. Runaway Wedding   36

9. Desperate for Love   41

10. Joni   47

11. The Best Gift   52

12. Loving Dad   58

13. A New Home   62

14. The Worst Day   67

15. Luke's Shenanigans   73

16. Love Again?   77

17. Luke's Troubles   80

18. Back to Reality   84

19. Serving God Together   88

20. Teen Slump   93

21. Arrested!   97

22. Wrecks and More Wrecks   102

23. Arrested Again   107

24. Does Luke Love Me?   113

25. Nightmare   118

26. Eulogy   126

27. God's Comfort   130

28. Preserving Memories   135

29. Justice   141

30. My Mistakes and Grief Process   146

31. Assurance   151

32. I Love You!   154

In Case You Missed It—Also by Tammy Horvath   159

Note to the Reader   162

DEDICATION

In Loving Memory of Luke Jacob Yuzwa
January 24, 1998–August 2, 2017
I was very blessed to have Luke in my life for the nineteen years God loaned him to me. He is now back with his Creator and finally at peace. I will forever love and miss him.

1. Gone!

Every morning when I rise from my bed, I notice all the places Luke is missing from. He's not hanging out in my spotless living room, making the cat jump for the toy just out of reach, making me laugh. He's not in his messy bedroom where his deodorant, razor, and cigarettes lie right where he left them.

He is gone.

On August 2, 2017—the day I'll never forget—a murderer's bullet ended my nineteen-year-old son's life. Why did God allow this to happen?

I never could have survived the following days, weeks, months, and years without God's deep love and comfort. And while I was angry a stranger would murder my son, I never once felt hatred for the killer. God's Word tells us:

"Do not repay anyone evil for evil. ... Do not take revenge, my dear friends." (Rom. 12:17, 19)

I chose to forgive my son's killer for what he took from me.

Throughout my life I've made so many mistakes undeserving of forgiveness, and yet I was forgiven. At fifteen, I rebelled against God and my parents to be with the charming twenty-four-year-old predator who would become my husband and the father of my son. Ignoring good advice and God's strong warnings, I left my difficult home situation, only to find that the man of my dreams was a clone of my alcoholic father, whom I had run away from.

My one joy in this nightmare was Luke. For years, I endured my husband's infidelity, alcoholism, abuse, and criminal activity until one night he was killed in a car crash. At twenty-eight years of age, I found myself widowed, a single mother to my very young child. The heavenly Father I'd rebelled against became my only hope.

Eighteen years later, just when my son reached the prime of his life, the unspeakable happened and he was gone.

The most unexpected thing took place when I faced my son's killer and told him directly that I forgave him. My heart broke for him—this total stranger who seemed little more than a boy himself. Through my pain, by God's grace, I felt a flood of love for my son's murderer. I wasn't just making a public declaration of forgiveness. Forgiveness flowed through every fiber of my soul. With it, came peace.

I had never thought of myself as a writer, but God had a different plan in calling me to write *Gone in an Instant: Losing My Son. Loving His Killer.* This book doesn't just chronicle the agonizing events of my son's death but follows my own journey to faith, forgiveness, love, and renewed hope. Ultimately, it's about how I learned to live each day to honor my son's memory and to serve God with the assurance that he will use my son's death for good, because that is what our heavenly Father does.

Forgiveness is not easy; it takes a lot of work, but the end result makes it all worthwhile.

Do you struggle to forgive but can't figure out how? Do you want to be free, once and for all, of all the things you haven't forgiven *yourself* for? Have you lost a loved one and can't find healing for your pain? Do you feel God has abandoned you or was never with you in the first place?

If so, you are the person for whom I wrote this book. As you read, may God comfort you with the comfort he has given me.

2. A MOTHER'S WORST NIGHTMARE

Wednesday, August 2, 2017, had been a hot and humid day. At 5:00 p.m., I'd just returned home from my job at a real estate office when the phone rang. I didn't recognize the number.

"Hey, Mom, can you come get me and give me a ride home?"

"Where are you and whose number are you calling from?"

Luke explained he was at the house of a friend in Old Conemaugh, a small borough about fifteen minutes from my home in Sidman, near Pittsburgh, Pennsylvania. "I need a ride home so I can pick up a few things. Then I need you to bring me back here."

Inwardly, I groaned. It had been a long, hard day at work. I was exhausted. Besides, Old Conemaugh was known for drug-dealing, youth gangs, and violent crime that exceeded the national average. Although Luke had placed his faith in Jesus Christ in his younger years, by his teens he'd started abusing drugs and alcohol and getting involved in drug-dealing behaviors that mirrored his birth father's.

On that day, I thought he had moved past that. He was working hard at odd jobs, hoping to save enough to move into his own place. But I still worried. When I tried to warn him about the people and places he visited, how dangerous his choices could become, he shrugged me off. He seemed to believe himself invincible. How could I get through to him? He was the most important person in this world to me, the reason I got out of bed every morning.

Nothing I said worked. As Luke reminded me often, he was an adult, and I couldn't control his behavior and choices.

Still, I put my foot down.

"If you want a ride home, I'll gladly come get you. But I'm not driving you back. You come home, you stay home."

"Never mind then. I'll just find another way."

Luke didn't sound upset, but I, a codependent who grew up with an alcoholic father, reacted as I usually did. I began apologizing. "Look, I'm sorry. It's just that it's been a long day, and I'm really tired."

"It's not a big deal," he cut in. Looking back, was he as weary of my need to feel needed, my exaggerated sense of responsibility, as I was? "I'll figure something out." He paused, then added more gently, "I love you, Mom."

"I love you too." I felt relief, happy he wasn't angry with me. As I would discover later, my caretaking had become compulsive and defeating, but I didn't see it then.

An hour later, I heard Luke enter the house. He bounded up the stairs, headed for his bedroom, and picked up whatever he needed. He ran downstairs and talked to his beloved cat before closing the front door behind him. I wanted to hug him and ask when he'd be home, but he came and left before I had finished in the bathroom.

Shortly after, my husband of fourteen years, Mike, arrived home from his job at the water company. The rest of the night went smoothly. We ate dinner while watching television, then headed to bed. Both tired, we slept soundly until our front doorbell rang.

Startled out of a dead sleep, I climbed out of bed and headed for the door in my nightgown. Who could possibly be at the door at this hour? Was it one of Luke's friends? I hurried. I didn't want the noise waking my husband.

Flipping on the porch light, I glanced out the door window. To my shock, I saw two uniformed police officers and another wearing civilian clothing. He carried a laptop that glowed brightly. Odd.

What brought them here? Why had they come? Had Luke been arrested? It wouldn't have been the first time. But on those occasions, law enforcement hadn't made house calls. My stomach clenched with foreboding.

Opening the door, an officer stepped forward. "May we come in?"

By now, Mike had heard the commotion. As the three men stepped inside, he joined us, looking as shocked and worried as I felt. As Mike escorted them to our kitchen, I rushed to our bedroom and put on my robe. By the time I returned, Mike had sunk into a seat at our kitchen table.

One of the officers turned to me. "Ma'am, could you please take a seat?" Numb, I just nodded.

"Is your name Tammy Horvath? Is Luke Yuzwa your son?"

"Yes, I'm his mother."

The man with the laptop came to the point. "We are sorry to inform you, ma'am, that your son Luke was shot and killed this evening in Old Conemaugh."

What? I started to shake. How could my son be dead? I hadn't had time to hug or say goodbye to him. Sobbing uncontrollably, my mind screamed, *Not again. First his father and now him!*

My voice shook. "Are you sure it's Luke?"

"He was with two of his friends. They positively identified him."

He leaned over and handed me a business card. The coroner. "I'll be able to give you more information once I've completed the autopsy."

I wanted to ask which friend had identified Luke, but I felt sick at heart, knowing I wouldn't have known them anyway. Secretive Luke never talked about his friends and rarely brought them around.

"Do you know who did it or why?"

"We already have a suspect," an officer said. "As to why we aren't sure yet unless it was a business deal gone wrong."

Holding my head in my hands, tears dripped down my face as I listened to the facts the officer knew. Luke had been hanging out at his friends' house when Tyrone, a young man in his twenties, showed up to buy drugs.

My heart sank. So Luke was still dealing drugs after all. How did I not know? I'd thought he was doing so much better. A lie. Luke had been filling capsules with THC oil extracted from marijuana and selling them on the street.

My head ached listening to the policemen recount the events leading up to Luke's death. Apparently, Tyrone didn't want to complete the deal inside, so he and Luke went outside and began walking along a dark road. When Luke bent down to get the pills from his backpack, Tyrone drew a gun. He took one step back and shot my son point-blank. He snatched Luke's backpack and ran.

"We've already located the suspect and have him in custody," the officer continued. "He's being charged with criminal homicide and robbery."

Nothing more could be said, but I had to know. "Did my son feel any pain?"

The coroner shook his head. "He was shot at point-blank range in the head and died instantly. So, no, he didn't feel anything. But again, we'll be doing an autopsy in the morning. If any other info emerges, I'll let you know."

Mike and I just sat there. In the backs of our minds, we always knew something like this could happen. Despite our warnings, Luke had chosen a dangerous lifestyle. But sitting at the kitchen table in the early morning hours, I didn't want to be right. I wanted my son back.

3. Dysfunctional

It was no surprise that I had puffy eyes and a body that refused to function. I was like a zombie, detached from my mind. Just going through the motions without any real awareness of anything happening around me. How was I going to get through this? Luke was my world, and now he was gone.

I can't imagine how any parent survives losing a child. My parents would've been devastated had they lost me. They were still teenagers when they married a few months after graduating from high school—Dad just nineteen, Mom not quite eighteen. Mom grew up attending church and Dad wanted to become a preacher one day. They read the Bible together and, after their marriage, attended a church just a block from their apartment in the small community of Beaverdale, Pennsylvania.

I was born the following spring. Being young and now with a family, my parents struggled financially. Mom found work as a stenographer for a year. My father worked in construction. His parents lived two miles away in Sidman, so Gram cared for me while Mom worked. My earliest memories include running around my grandparents' big backyard.

Sometimes Dad got laid off. Discouraged, he started drinking. While Mom wouldn't allow him to drink in our house, I can't remember a time when he didn't come home drunk and I often heard my parents arguing about it. Even at a young age, Mom told me getting drunk was a sin. She regularly read the Bible to me, including the apostle Paul's admonition in Ephesians 5:18 not to "get drunk on wine, which leads to debauchery. Instead, be filled with the Spirit." I was worried about my dad because I didn't understand what the word debauchery meant, so I didn't ask, and I was upset with Mom for sharing these difficult verses with me.

Yet my dad had his good moments too. One day when I was not quite four years old, I heard a soft barking in our living room. When I ran into the room, I found my dad with an adorable black-and-white male puppy. Dad said he wanted to make his little girl happy. I was ecstatic.

I fell in love with that puppy and named him Jinx. That was the best day ever. Jinx was my constant companion, slept with me at night, and comforted me when my parents fought. Sadly, I wasn't old enough to potty train the puppy, and Mom worked long hours while Dad was always absent, so Jinx wasn't allowed inside anymore because he kept having accidents. Too young to understand why I couldn't have my best friend with me anymore, I was heartbroken and sobbed hysterically.

About a year later, we moved into a two-bedroom house just a few blocks from our original apartment. Our home sat in a valley amid vibrant hills next to a roaring creek. Soon after moving into our new home, my sister Jamie was born. Wanting both of us dedicated to God, my parents had us baptized. Though my father professed his faith when he was younger, he'd never been baptized, so he asked the pastor to baptize him too.

I was old enough to remember. On the way home, we stopped at a fast-food restaurant, a special treat on our tight budget, to celebrate this wonderful day. But a few months later, Dad quit going to church with the rest of us.

One summer, Dad took my mom, sister, and me to South Carolina to spend a week with my maternal grandmother. We went swimming and to a seafood buffet. But the trip was memorable because Dad spent a lot of time with us.

Other good memories of Dad include fishing and watching him build a cabin in our backyard for me to play in. One Saturday afternoon, he asked if I wanted to learn how to shoot his rifle. Excited to do anything with my dad, I immediately agreed. He collected the rifle and a box of cartridges and drove us to a shooting range near our house. There he pointed out the target I was supposed to shoot at and handed me the gun. Since I had no idea how to use it, I just looked at him confused.

Knowing his short fuse, I was afraid to ask any questions. Instead, I asked if he'd shoot first. Watching him carefully, I then copied what he'd done. I succeeded in shooting the rifle but didn't hit the target. He let me try a few more times, then said it was time to leave. I was overjoyed to have spent time with my dad.

"Dad, thank you for showing me how to shoot," I told him. "I love you."

Though he made no response to my declaration, it almost did feel that he loved me. So I added that day to my mental memory book to savor forever.

These memories mattered because the older I became, the more aware I became that my dad was different from my friends' fathers. They were affectionate, always around. They loved their daughters and told them. I'd never heard those words from my father. He never complimented me. In contrast, he yelled whenever I did anything he'd told me not to do. The words he spewed at me made me feel like I never did anything right.

Sometimes, I'd ask him if a girlfriend could sleep over. Sometimes he said yes. Other times he made his permission conditional. Once, he told me a friend could stay over if I drank a whole glass of buttermilk, which he knew I hated. Pinching my nose, I drank the whole thing, only to be told my friend wouldn't be sleeping over anyway. These head games should've made me hate him, but I couldn't. He was my dad and I wanted him to love me, so I fought harder to earn that love.

Occasionally Dad played card games with us. Craving his love and approval, I'd insist on sitting next to him. Being a child, I'd inadvertently tilt my hand in such a way that he could see my cards. This made Dad furious. Sometimes he'd just yell at me. But if I made the mistake again, he'd get up without warning and storm out of the house, leaving me crying and Mom speechless.

One night at dinner, I did something that upset him enough he flipped the table upside-down. Still, nothing my dad did stopped me from loving him and trying as hard as possible to please him and win his love.

All that said, if I wanted to buy something or go anywhere, Dad was my go-to. Since he was rarely home, it would have been natural to ask Mom. But her default was almost always no. When Mom said no, that usually meant that dad would say yes. It was almost as if he said yes just to overrule her. So I'd wait until Dad came home drunk to ask him. Under the influence, he'd say yes 99 percent of the time. Of course, Mom wasn't happy about me going behind her back, which I could understand, but I did it anyway.

Mom was the complete opposite to my alcoholic, absent dad. Religious and strict, she did her best to raise my sister and me to be godly young women as King Solomon advised in the Old Testament book of Proverbs:

"Start children off on the way they should go, and even when they are old they will not turn from it." (Prov. 22:6)

Mom would come into our bedroom each night to read Jamie and me a Bible story, then say a prayer with the two of us before kissing us goodnight. Despite our almost-five-year age difference, my sister and I had a close relationship. We were also quite similar in appearance with the same blond hair and general features, though my eyes were blue like Dad's and hers were brown like Mom's.

Although Dad no longer attended church, Mom always made sure Jamie and I were there each Sunday. We only had one car, which Dad monopolized all week. But on Sunday mornings, he let Mom use the car to drive to church while he lounged around the house.

Mom also had Jamie and me memorize countless Bible verses set each week by our church. On Sundays, the pastor would ask for volunteers to stand up and recite that week's verse in front of the entire congregation. I never raised my hand but did occasionally get called on. Thanks to Mom's strict coaching, Jamie and I always knew the verses well enough not to embarrass ourselves or her.

Now that we were old enough, Mom also made sure we learned to do chores around the house. After we finished, she inspected everything. If we didn't get something clean enough, we had to redo it until it was perfect. I rejected and rebelled against her extremely high standards, suspicious her purpose was merely to make me miserable. After one Sunday dinner, I had to rewash the dishes six times. She'd run her finger along the edge of the floor when we cleaned it. If she found any dust or dirt, we had to re-clean the whole floor. Growing up, our relationship was riddled with tension. But, as an adult, I came to appreciate knowing how to keep a spotless house and enjoy the many compliments my friends give when they see my home.

The church we attended had a "hellfire-and-brimstone" style of preaching. Every Sunday, the preacher would talk about how bad hell was going to be and the eternal torment we could expect if we didn't ask Jesus into our hearts and let God have control of our lives. As with my dad, I heard little mention of God as a heavenly Father who loves us rather than a God of judgment to be feared.

At the age of thirteen, I asked Jesus into my heart as my Savior. I was completely sincere, and I know he entered my heart and gave me new life as the apostle Paul described:

"Therefore, if anyone is in Christ, the new creation has come: The old has gone, the new is here!" (2 Cor. 5:17)

That said, let me be honest that my motivations were less a desire to follow Jesus as my Savior and daily Lord of my life than my utter dread and terror of being sent to hell to spend an eternity in suffering and torment. Not until much later in life would I learn that our God is a God of love, not a God of condemnation (John 3:16–17). That truth would completely change my life.

Meantime, nothing much changed about the way I was living my life or my own attitudes toward my family, daily life, and God himself. In fact, my attitude toward God was becoming increasingly bitter and angry. Around this time, my maternal grandmother gave Mom a used car. This made it easier for us to go to church since we no longer had to ask Dad for his car. It also allowed Mom to get a job in Johnstown, a half-hour drive away, doing clerical work for an insurance company.

This left me babysitting my younger sister and learning to cook. Mom left me a detailed note each day, and I followed all her instructions. Dad had recently started attending church with us again and occasionally read the Bible with us. One day when both parents were out, I went into their bedroom. Snooping through my dad's built-in desk, I was astonished to find a pile of poems about God with his signature at the bottom.

I loved writing poetry too, so I was amazed to discover I'd received this talent from my dad. The poems were exquisite. Among my favorites is the following:

Satan stands at the gate of sin,
and only evil can pass within.
Satan sits at the gate of sin,
he curses all that must come in.
For these people so loved the world,
forever to hell they will be hurled.
They had a chance from God above,
but they chose the world, not God's love.

I was even more astonished at the theme of these poems. They demonstrated that Dad really did have faith and yearned to follow God despite his struggle with alcoholism. Sadly, something happened a few months later that hardened his feelings toward church. He'd again stopped attending with Mom, Jamie, and me. The church elders tried to encourage him to come back, telling him if he didn't begin attending regularly, he'd be stripped of his membership.

After several warnings, Dad chose to remain home, so he was eventually excommunicated from our church. The rationale given by the church elders was that by excommunicating him, they hoped his conscience would be burdened enough to make him repent and return to church. Instead, it just made him angry. It made me even angrier. I hated the church for what they were doing to my dad. And this made me feel like I hated God too.

Looking back, Luke's story began long before he was ever born. Everything that happened to me in my childhood affected the way I raised Luke. My lack of being a responsible parent. Not knowing if my parents loved me. Not feeling God's love. Every detail of my upbringing shaped me into the mom that I would one day become—the codependent mom who wouldn't let her child think for himself and expected him to be perfect like she strived to be.

4. First Loves

My growing anger against God as well as my despondency that I would never manage to earn my own father's love affected my state of mind and choices as I moved into my high school years, especially as I became more interested in boys. I'd always been an excellent student, receiving mostly As and Bs on my report card. So, in ninth grade, I began tutoring other students during my study hall period.

By this point, even though my mom and I were very close in my younger years, we were now constantly fighting. She limited me to three phone calls per day with no more than ten minutes per call. I had to wash dishes or do some other chore every evening. I didn't like having to clean something repeatedly because it wasn't up to her expectations. She also grounded me any time I got a grade below a B, which was rare. A C was supposed to be average, so why should I have to be above average? I just wanted to be like everyone else.

She also grounded me if I was even one minute late getting home from a friend's house. In my opinion, her rules were too strict. In my adulthood, I eventually learned that Mom's own mother had been extremely strict, to the point of physical abuse. At the time, my anger and frustration reached the point I couldn't stand to be in the house with her. I wish I could go back in time when Mom used to braid my hair and watch TV with me, but those days were a long time ago, and so was the peace.

Since Dad was never home to take my side as he did every time my mom said no, sometimes I'd walk to the bar to sit with him. In a town as small as ours, the bartender never cared that I was underage. Dad would buy me a soda while he drank something alcoholic. Dad introduced me to his friends as his beautiful little girl. I treasured those moments when I had him all to myself instead of sharing with my mother and sister. I also cherished the times when he'd come home drunk in the middle of the night and shout out to ask if anyone wanted pizza, which he'd bring home from the bar. I was always the first to enter the kitchen.

Near the end of ninth grade, a good-looking young man was sitting on a porch one morning while I was walking to the bus stop. He had jet-black hair, big blue eyes, and a dark tan. He was there every day and he always stared at me. Although I tried to keep my head down as I passed by, it was hard to resist staring back.

One morning, he called out to me, asking my name. When I paused to tell him, he responded that his name was Troy. He'd just moved from Louisiana for work and lived with his dad and another friend who'd come with him. He asked if I'd be free to talk with him after school. At barely fifteen years of age, I was too trusting and naïve, but he was so gorgeous I couldn't resist. I told him I'd see him later.

All that day during classes, I could think of nothing else. Finally, when school ended, I rushed to his porch. My parents were both working that day, so I had at least an hour to hang out with Troy before I needed to get home. As I sat down, he offered me a beer.

I did wrestle briefly with my conscience, but over the years I had developed a bad habit of acting without thinking. I knew neither my parents nor God would want me there in the first place, and God would definitely not want me drinking beer. But I was still angry with God so I accepted the beer. After all, my dad never bothered to show me any attention and here was this gorgeous older guy who seemed to really enjoy being around me.

Troy told me he was nineteen. I told him I was fifteen. He didn't seem to care that he'd given alcohol to an underage schoolgirl. Of course at nineteen, he was technically underage too, since the drinking age was twenty-one.

After chatting awhile, he asked if I wanted to go out to a movie on Saturday. Without thinking, I immediately said yes even though I'd have to lie to my mom. I left without finishing the beer. In truth, it didn't taste good. But I didn't want to tell him that.

On Saturday, I asked Mom if I could go to the movies with Tracy, a longtime friend who lived up the road from us. Mom said I could go as long as I finished my housework first. I rushed to get it done, then walked over to Troy's apartment, just a block from our house. He was already outside waiting for me beside a white truck. I was relieved to see that it had tinted windows, so no one would be able to see me riding around with a stranger and tell my parents.

We decided to skip the movie and just drove around for hours. I pointed out a few of my favorite restaurants and the local bowling alley. When we arrived back at his apartment, he leaned over, and through the longest black lashes I've ever seen, I became mesmerized by his big blue eyes. Then he kissed me. He invited me inside, but I declined and headed home. He yelled out for me to stop over any time. I just smiled and kept walking.

When I got home, Mom asked how the movie was. I told her it was good and headed to my room. I couldn't stop thinking about Troy. He seemed like such a nice guy.

The next day, I was outside hanging around with a neighbor girl, Patty, who was a couple of years older than me. I told her about Troy, and we decided to walk over to his apartment to see if he was home. Troy answered the door and invited us in. He also introduced us to the friend, whose name was Keenan, who'd come with him from Louisiana.

Patty and Keenan quickly decided to go for a walk, leaving Troy and me alone. It wasn't long before he started kissing me. Within a few more dates, I'd lost my virginity to Troy. Once again, my conscience told me this was wrong, and by now, I thought that God must hate me. But I felt so deeply in love with Troy, and I wanted him to love me as much as I loved him.

I know now that I rebelled against my parents, Mom for being so strict and Dad for not loving me. I blamed God because Dad couldn't be a member of our church anymore. So full of anger against everyone I put myself in danger, but I didn't care what happened to me or how my actions affected anyone around me.

Troy had a major drinking problem, just like my dad. But he also showed me the attention and warmth I craved, which made me want to be with him all the more. After we'd dated several months, I asked Troy if he'd be willing to talk to Dad and see if my parents would let me marry him. His current job would soon be over, and he'd be going back to Louisiana. Like sunshine in the midst of a hailstorm, I drowned in my love for him and I was determined to go with him.

What I didn't know was that Troy already knew my dad because they'd become drinking buddies at the bar. Whatever Troy said, Dad came home in a drunken fit of rage. As he crossed the room with clenched fists, I could see his angry expression directed at me. My instinct said, "Run," but my paralyzed body wouldn't listen to my brain. My teary eyes locked on Dad's bloodshot eyes when he slapped me across the face. My only thought was, *What did I do?* His face was distorted with rage. My cheek stung. My body violently shook as I tried to run.

Yanking me by my long hair, Dad pulled me back to him. I cried for Mom to help me, but she sat there stunned with her mouth hanging open. Dad's hands wrapped around my throat so tight that I felt his pulse. I tried to beg him to stop, but I couldn't make a sound. He lifted me so high into the air my feet were off the floor; I was desperate for him to stop. *Dad had never been angry with me before to the point of hitting me. I was Daddy's little girl. Why was he doing this?* Terror consumed me and the blood drained from my face and limbs. Weak from fear, I gave up my struggle and lost control of my bladder when he released me. Embarrassed, I fell to the floor like a rag doll. Meanwhile, Mom had gone ballistic, trying to stop my dad from hurting me.

Dad bellowed, "If you want to marry Troy, go ahead and marry him. Now get out of my sight because I can't stand to look at you!" After Dad walked away, Mom made sure I wasn't seriously hurt, then ordered me not to leave the house.

That was the last time Dad ever hit me. Monday morning, when I walked to the bus stop for school, I was shocked to see that Troy's truck was no longer parked outside his dad's apartment. His friend Keenan was sitting on the porch, so I asked where Troy was.

"He went home to Louisiana."

"When will he be back?"

"He isn't coming back. He got a new job on a cruise ship."

My heart broke at Keenan's words.

That fall, I entered tenth grade. I got into a huge fight with my mom. With my typical impulsiveness, I decided I'd had enough. Packing a bag, I took the bus to school and told my friends I was running away.

Looking back, I know how stupid I was, the danger into which I put myself, and how badly I must have scared my parents. But at that moment, I couldn't take it anymore—the daily screaming matches with Mom, and Dad not showing an iota of concern for me. He was like fire and ice, giving me whatever I begged for when he was drunk, then treating me like I could do no good the rest of the time. My house felt like there was no love in it at all. At that moment, I'd rather have been dead than keep living with my parents.

Did Luke feel the same way about me? Was he sick of the screaming matches we had every day?

Leaving the school, I hiked to the highway, where I hitchhiked a ride south from a truck driver. He spent the entire first leg of the trip trying to talk me into returning home. He even offered to turn around and drive me all the way back home. He eventually stopped to buy me lunch, dragging out our time together in the hope that I'd change my mind. But I insisted on continuing my journey.

After I left the restaurant, I caught a ride with another trucker. I told him I was eighteen and hitchhiking south to see my grandparents. But, in truth, I planned to try to find Troy in Louisiana. That first night, I slept in the front seat of the trucker's cab to save what little money I had while he slept in the truck bed. By the next afternoon, we'd reached Tennessee.

That evening, I told the truth about my age. I guess God was still in my mind and heart, even if I didn't want him there. The trucker was furious at the deception. He immediately drove me to a hotel, where he made me get out of the truck.

By now, I was getting nervous, even scared. I only had a little over a hundred dollars to my name, and by the time I checked into the hotel, I'd spent most of that. Picking up the phone, I called a friend and asked if he and his dad could drive down and get me.

"What's going on?" Ken demanded, concerned. "Why would you run away? Where are you?"

I explained briefly. After a short discussion with his dad, Ken informed me they were coming to get me and to stay where I was until they arrived. But I'd barely settled in to wait when a knock came at the hotel room door. It was the police. Next thing I knew, they'd hauled me off to juvenile detention.

I found out later that Ken's mom had called my parents to let them know where I was. Afraid I might run off again, my parents called the Tennessee police. At that time, Beaverdale was locked down by a major blizzard. But Dad immediately got into his car and headed to Tennessee to get me.

All my life I wondered if my dad ever really loved me. But as I write this, I realize that dropping everything to drive seven hundred miles on icy roads through a blizzard to get me was his way of showing me that he did love me.

When he reached Tennessee, the detention center released me into his custody. We headed back home into a full-blown blizzard. Dad hardly said a word to me, not that he ever talked much unless he was drinking. But I could see how much my running away had scared him and his relief that his little girl was okay.

5. LOVE OF MY LIFE

I turned sixteen that spring. Pudge, a good friend, lived a block from my house, right across the street from a bar. We'd swing on her front porch for hours, talking about boys and our dreams for the future. We could hear loud music and even smell cigarette smoke every time someone opened the bar's front door.

One hot evening in May, Pudge and I noticed a classy blue Pontiac Firebird sports car in the bar parking lot. With my usual impulsiveness, I strolled over to check it out. The windows were open and I could smell pine air freshener inside. A pack of cigarettes sat on the console. I headed back across the street.

Shortly thereafter, a tall handsome man in his twenties strolled out of the bar and climbed into the Firebird. The engine roared as he accelerated out of the parking lot. He stared at me. He had longish dark-brown hair and a mustache.

About five minutes later, I saw the Firebird heading back toward Pudge's house, so I put out my thumb in the hitchhiking gesture. The Firebird pulled over. Leaning into the passenger window, I asked, "Will you take me for a ride?"

He smiled widely. "Sure, hop in."

After riding for five minutes through some very windy roads, we pulled onto a grassy lot next to a creepy-looking cemetery. I felt nervous, not because I was in a car alone with a stranger, but because I already was attracted to this guy.

He said his name was Tony Yuzwa. He was twenty-four years old and lived in an apartment building his parents owned just three blocks from my house. His parents operated a restaurant in the same building. I'd probably seen him in passing but never really noticed him until he acquired his beautiful blue Firebird. So I guess one could say it was the car, not the man, that hooked the girl.

After talking for a few minutes, he asked if I'd like to go out sometime. I was well aware my parents would have a fit if they knew. But I immediately said yes. The following day was the last school day of the year and would only be for an hour. We agreed that once I was free, I'd head over to a nearby pizzeria, where he'd be waiting in the parking lot. He leaned over to kiss me, which gave me butterflies in my stomach, then drove me back to Pudge's house.

Deciding to go out with a much older man I'd met coming out of a bar after an hour's acquaintance was stupid, even for my foolish, impulsive sixteen-year-old naivete, and turned out to be the worst mistake I ever made. But when I look back, trying to understand why I did it, I realize that, like Troy, Tony reminded me of my dad. He was handsome and charming—and a drinker.

I would soon find out he was far more and worse. But at the time, I desperately wanted to be loved. I wanted a man who would marry me and take me away from my miserable homelife. I knew the difference between right and wrong and that going out with Tony was wrong. But I was beyond caring.

Nor did I care if my actions hurt my mom or dad. I tried not to care that I was disobeying and angering God. I prayed every night and apologized to God for everything I did wrong, but I couldn't stop doing it. Finding someone to love me seemed far more important. That God might just be that someone never entered my mind because I still had no idea our God is a God of love. As far as I was concerned, God was just a punisher.

The following morning, I asked Mom if I could stay overnight at my friend's house. Bonnie lived on another school bus route. Mom agreed and wrote a note that would allow me to ride Bonnie's bus. Of course, I had no intention of doing so.

The only activity on that last morning of school was reporting to homeroom to receive our report cards. I discovered I'd received all As and Bs except for a D in algebra. I knew I'd be grounded half the summer if I went home with a D. Since the grades were written in pen, I grabbed a pen of the same color and carefully shaped the D into a B. Since my first three-quarter grades in algebra had been Bs, my overall average was still decent, so my parents wouldn't notice what I'd done.

The dismissal bell finally rang. I headed to the pizzeria. But there was no sign of the blue Firebird, so I began to get nervous. What would I do if Tony didn't show up?

I would soon learn that Tony was always late for everything. When I stepped into the pizzeria parking lot, I saw the blue Firebird racing down the street. Tony pulled in alongside me, smiling as though he was looking at an angel. My heart fluttered as I smiled back.

After getting in the car, Tony offered me a beer. This wasn't a good idea, but I didn't want to appear schoolgirlish, so I drank it. We drove around for a few hours, getting to know each other. Then he took me to a pizza place. I ordered a Mountain Dew while he asked for a Diet Pepsi. I thought that odd since he was so tall and thin. I later learned he always drank diet soda because he had type 1 diabetes.

After we'd eaten, he asked if I'd be interested in camping for the night. I was enthralled enough with him by now to agree immediately. I learned that his suggestion was less romantic and more that he didn't have much money. A cloud of fine brown dust swirled through the car as we drove on the back dirt roads looking for a place to pitch a tent while there was still enough light to do so.

The tall trees emitted a strong pine smell where we parked. As he set the tent up, which surprisingly was already in the trunk, birds sang joyously in the shaded trees overhead. The breeze coming off the trees was just enough to make the hot day comfortable. It was so relaxing out in the middle of nowhere; I didn't want to leave. After setting up the tent, he laid out a sleeping bag inside. When we climbed back into the car, he popped a cassette into the cassette player. He sang a song called "The End," written by Jim

Morrison, lead vocalist of the rock band The Doors, who'd died unexpectedly at twenty-seven.

I'd fantasized about being serenaded. My heart melted at Tony's romantic gesture. Even with the enchantment of his voice, I wondered why he'd chosen a song written about a painful breakup with imagery of death, killing, and a hopeless end. I would learn too late what a warning sign that was.

We left the campsite and went to the movies. After leaving the theater, someone cut in front of our car on the highway. Tony swore and pulled alongside the culprit's car. He reached under his black leather vest and pulled out a .38 Special. I screamed, "What are you doing with a gun? Surely you don't plan on shooting the driver?" I was scared more than I had ever been in my life. Begging Tony, "Please put it away. What if he has a gun and shoots back. I don't want to die." He slowed the car and put the gun back in its holster—what a relief!

Back at the tent we stumbled in the darkness. I was so nervous lying on the sleeping bag I didn't think I'd be able to fall asleep. Suddenly, I felt something brush across my foot.

"Tony! There's something in the tent!"

Tony shone a flashlight around but didn't see anything.

"I want to leave."

"Are you sure?" he asked.

"Yes."

I waited in the car while he packed everything up. Sitting there in the dark, I asked myself what I was doing out there with a man I'd just met. I knew how unhappy God had to be with me. But Tony was a dream come true to me, and I quit trying to control where my emotions were leading me. I knew I would be physically involved with him before our date ended.

When Tony began driving, I fell asleep. The next thing I knew, it was morning. Glancing over, I saw Tony asleep in the driver's seat. I looked around to see we were parked next to the creepy cemetery where he'd taken me for a ride when I first met him the day before.

Waking up, Tony looked over at me. "Good morning, Sweetie."

At his endearment, I melted. After surrendering my body to him, I asked Tony who owned the grassy lot. It belonged to his family. He planned to

build a house there someday and have a wife and kids. That sounded wonderful too. Birds were chirping, the sun shining brightly. It was going to be
a beautiful day. As I looked into Tony's smiling brown eyes, I daydreamed.
Could this man be the one who would really love me and free me from my
pain?

6. True Colors

Tony dropped me off at my friend's house since I'd told Mom I'd be there. Bonnie was shocked to see me. Tony extended his huge scarred hand to Bonnie and firmly shook her hand. I explained about my date with Tony, and as a good friend, Bonnie agreed not to give away my secret and let me call my mom to pick me up. Before leaving, I told Bonnie that Tony is the man I will marry. When I got into the car, Mom asked if I'd had fun. I lied again, telling her that Bonnie and I had watched a movie.

I called Tony as soon as I got home to ask if we could meet the next day. I always had to call Tony since his voice was clearly that of a man, not a high school boy. My parents would have asked too many questions if he'd called.

We agreed to meet at a nearby abandoned coal mine. Leaving home a little after lunch, I raced to meet Tony, breathlessly cursing my white strappy sandals that threatened to trip me headlong with every step I took. Trees had grown up on the paths, which offered lots of shade for strolling. Local kids often rode their bikes on the trails.

I climbed a small hill to reach the mine entrance where we'd agreed to meet. I saw no sign of Tony, so I sat on a boulder to wait. About ten minutes later, I spotted him walking toward me, smoking a cigarette. The moment he saw me, a smile lit his eyes. My heart melted. We spent a few hours planning our next rendezvous.

By this point, my conscience kept wrestling with me for being physically involved with Tony, but I was also desperate to please him. I craved him like an addiction, and I worried that I'd never see him again if I didn't keep him happy. As with Troy, I was clinging desperately to that feeling of being someone's chosen one. I didn't understand then how utterly wrong it was for a twenty-four-year-old man to be pursuing a sixteen-year-old schoolgirl. Or that when an older man dates an immature adolescent, he isn't looking for a healthy, loving adult relationship.

Tony certainly knew I had none of his street smarts or worldly experience as he quickly nicknamed me Dingee, short for "dingbat," meaning a silly, empty-headed person. At the time, I was so enthralled with him I didn't even mind the implied insult. In truth, I did tend to babble when I got nervous, which made me seem even younger than my sixteen years. When I questioned why an older, streetwise man like Tony would want to be with me, he'd laugh and tell me I was a breath of fresh air.

That Friday, Tony invited me to accompany him to a party some friends were throwing in the woods. I was so excited I spent an hour on my hair and makeup, determined to make a good impression on Tony's friends, who I assumed would also be a lot older than me. I snuck out to wait for him at the coal mine entrance where we'd met before.

When Tony arrived, I climbed into the Firebird. The interior was spotless. He told me how he earned money detailing vehicles. He'd spend most of a day thoroughly cleaning them for fifty dollars a vehicle. That was good money at a time when the minimum wage was just over three dollars an hour.

The Firebird's gas gauge was on empty. At the gas station, Tony put in a meager two dollars' worth of gas. I later learned that his nickname was Two-Buck Tony and that the Firebird's gas gauge was always on empty. Tony had also earned the nickname Gangster, but more on that later.

When we arrived at the party, a large group of people were sitting on logs around a fire. I noticed immediately that all of them were years older than me. Someone handed me a cold beer. Again, no one seemed concerned that I was underage. A car stereo was blasting music by The Doors, Tony's favorite rock band.

Later, Tony asked if I wanted to drive the Firebird. I was thrilled to get behind the wheel. As we sped down the highway, Tony kept telling me to go faster. When I finally looked down at the speedometer, I discovered I was going one hundred in a fifty-five miles per hour zone. The wind in my hair, the power underneath me, and the control of it all in my hands was an exhilarating experience I'd never forget. I'm just thankful the highway patrol didn't pull us over.

Tony loved to discuss profound ideas as we drove around. He was interested in astral projection and the meaning behind Jim Morrison's lyrics "The End," the song he sang to me on our first date. I was impressed at his deep thinking and wanted to educate myself about anything Tony liked. I bought books on these topics. I also bought The Doors albums, and my nightly ritual now included listening to "The End" and focusing on the words.

By this time, I'd fallen far harder for Tony than I ever had for Troy. I was already fantasizing about marrying him. He showed me so much attention and made me feel loved when I was with him, as I'd never experienced with my dad or anyone else. I reveled in his description of building a house on his family's land and having a few kids. With Tony, I could finally have the perfect family I'd always longed for.

Subconsciously, I had the idea that if I married Tony and was no longer living in sin, God wouldn't stay angry with me. I also wanted to get out of my miserable home situation so badly I was willing to do anything. Mom and I were still fighting constantly, and in part at least, I wanted to hurt my mom by defying her to be with a man she'd never allow me to date.

I saw Tony as much as I could the rest of that summer. That fall, I started eleventh grade. Though I'd worked hard to keep my grades up, this was only to keep from being grounded as I hated school. I decided to switch to a vocational school where I majored in marketing and sales. My one goal now was to turn eighteen so I'd legally be an adult and could leave home for good.

Now that I was back in school, I didn't have time to see Tony as often. But every day at lunchtime, I'd race out of class to grab one of two phones available to students. Tony and I talked all through lunch. I asked Mom if I could join a bowling league that met Friday nights. She agreed, which allowed me to see Tony every Friday night.

Of course, we didn't go bowling but to a club where we played in a pool league. I knew nothing about pool, but Tony taught me quite a lot and was an excellent player himself. He'd won trophies as the best player in the league for the last three years.

Then one weekend, Tony asked me to hook up his friend with one of my girlfriends for a double date. My friend Patty liked to party, so I invited her. The four of us went out drinking, which had become a habit every time I was with Tony. I'd come to realize that Tony couldn't have a good time without getting drunk. This reminded me starkly of my dad, but instead of being a warning, it made me want to help him. Maybe my loving influence could get him to stop drinking and become a better person.

In the meantime, I was still compelled to do whatever Tony wanted so he wouldn't decide to leave me. The four of us started a game of poker. But we were soon making out, Tony with me, and Patty with his friend. Then Tony suggested we swap partners. I was not okay with this, but I didn't want to come across as lame, and I was pretty drunk as well, so I didn't resist. Tony was fully into kissing my friend Patty.

I shoved Tony's friend away. Lashing out at Tony I yelled, "What is wrong with you that you can make out with my friend in front of me?" And what was wrong with me that I could love a man who could behave like this?

I know now God was giving me a strong warning of what was ahead before I got in too deep. In fact, God gave me many chances to walk away. But I just wouldn't listen. Instead, I blocked God out of my thoughts, and that would cause my life to plummet into one disaster after another.

About a month later, Tony asked me again if I'd bring a girlfriend along for another friend named Curt. This time, I said no. When he picked me up, he'd brought his friend along anyway. Curt was about Tony's age and had recently been discharged from the army.

Tony had bought me a pair of four-inch-heeled black leather boots, a leather skirt, and a black Harley Davidson tank-top, which he insisted I put on. That entire evening, he had the three of us walk into each bar we visited with Curt on one side of me and Tony on the other, my arms looped through theirs. I knew I looked like some kind of floozy, but I was so in love with Tony I couldn't bring myself to protest. What if I refused and he left me?

Later in the evening, the fall winds began to blow and autumn leaves fell into the bar's gutter. So did I. Tony started kissing me. Then he told me to kiss Curt too because he was lonely and depressed after his army discharge. I didn't want to, but once again, I obediently followed Tony's commands. That night, I relived the moment too many times as my tears drenched my pillow. Unfortunately, that wasn't the last time Tony pushed me on other men. It hurt my feelings, but I didn't know what to do about it without the risk of losing his love.

One night when Tony was away, one of the men he'd forced me to kiss stopped by and kissed me. Tony walked in on the kiss and totally lost it. He threw the man outside and yelled at me. Since that day, I never had to kiss another man for him, though I saw Tony riding around with two girls in his car several times. He claimed he was just giving them a ride somewhere, but it happened too often for me to believe him.

7. A Marriage Proposal

In December, after several months of dating, Tony took me to an elegant restaurant. I didn't care for fancy places and was shocked by the prices. I was nervous that some of my parents' friends might spot us together. But when Tony had money, he liked to impress me with extravagant gestures. I didn't want to disappoint him, so I tried to relax as we ordered our drinks and meals.

Suddenly, Tony got down on one knee. My face turned bright red as the entire restaurant turned to stare at us.

"Sweetie, you are my angel and make my life great. Will you marry me?"

Of course, I said yes. There wasn't a doubt in my mind I wanted to marry him more than anything else in the world.

Tony slid a ring with a beautiful diamond on my finger. The entire restaurant cheered and clapped. I was embarrassed and worried someone might report what had just happened to my parents. But Tony always reveled in being the center of attention. That I was only sixteen years old didn't seem to concern him in the least. But I forgot everyone, except for Tony when the power and intensity of Tony's kiss crashed over me with more force than any hurricane could. My face was pure red when he pulled away.

Since my parents didn't know I was dating Tony, hiding the ring from them would be difficult. But I did my best, only wearing it at school and when I was with Tony. Things went great for a couple months. Tony was still living in his parents' apartment building in a one-room apartment with a shared bathroom down the hall. He had gotten rid of the Firebird due to engine trouble. Seeing it gone really upset me.

One night, I snuck out through a window after my parents went to sleep and walked to Tony's apartment. I fell asleep. When I woke up, it was 5:30 a.m. Freaking out, I shook Tony awake. Dad was an early riser, so he'd probably be awake already. I ran home. Climbing back in through the window, I walked into the kitchen. On the counter was my driver's permit, cut into pieces.

I'd been caught. Bursting into tears, I climbed out the window again and ran back to Tony's apartment. He'd already gone back to sleep. Waking him, I said I needed to run away. If my parents could ground me for a C on my report card, I figured they'd never let me out again once they knew about Tony. I couldn't live without him.

Tony tried to calm me down, insisting that running away wasn't the answer. He told me to go home and that everything would be okay. I told my parents that Tony and I were in love and engaged to be married. Mom replied that Tony had broken the law by having a relationship with me when I was underage.

I got grounded, and Mom pressed charges against Tony. I cried and pleaded with her not to punish Tony for my own choices. She finally dropped the more serious charges, but Tony still had to appear in court and pay fines. He told me we'd need to cool things for a while. A short time later, he asked me to return my engagement ring. That's when I found out that the ring had been purchased on a loan in his brother's name and Tony could no longer keep up with the payments.

This broke my heart since I truly loved him and, just like his high-priced choice of restaurants, I hadn't needed a fancy ring he couldn't afford. All I wanted was his love, but I no longer had confidence he really loved me.

I dropped the ring off on my way home from school. I noticed he was now driving a small, well-used red Toyota Corolla and wished he hadn't gotten rid of the Firebird. The following day on the bus ride to school, a commotion broke out with kids rushing from their seats to the right-side windows.

"What's going on?" I called out.

"Come look at this wrecked car," someone responded excitedly.

When I looked out the window, I just about fainted. A huge boulder had caved in the whole front of Tony's car. I saw hair and blood on the shattered front windshield. I started shaking from shock. Since Tony never wore a seat belt, I was worried he'd been killed.

With tear-filled eyes and shaking hands, I struggled to use the pay phone at school to call his parents' restaurant, but no one answered. Now I was really concerned, but the bell rang, and I had to rush to class. I barely paid attention through my morning classes. When the lunch bell rang, I raced to the phone. Tony's mom assured me he was okay but sleeping.

That evening, Tony told me he'd stayed out late with Curt and had fallen asleep at the wheel. I'd already found out he had diabetes and took insulin shots. Diabetes and alcohol don't mix well, and staying out all night certainly couldn't help. That was the last time Tony spoke to me for quite a while.

In March, my parents finally let me get my driver's license since I'd be seventeen in another month. I passed my test on the first try. I was overjoyed. Dad had bought me an old green Chevy Impala for two hundred dollars, and I immediately took it for a drive. Even though I had my own car, I didn't have much more freedom because my curfews were strict.

I'd occasionally see Tony driving around town in an older white Cadillac that belonged to his parents. He usually had girls in the car, which was extremely painful for me. I understood why he wouldn't want to see me after Mom pressed charges, but that didn't stop me from loving him with every breath I took.

I dated a boy my own age for a few months, hoping this would help me get over Tony. But as soon as I developed feelings for my new boyfriend, Tony called to say he wanted to see me. I was so confused. Did he want to get back together? If not, what *did* he want?

"We need to talk in person," he said.

"Fine," I responded.

He picked me up in his parents' Cadillac. It was so hot you could feel the heat coming through the windows. After parking on his parents' land by the cemetery, we sat on a rock in the shade from the trees. Chirping birds relaxed my stressed body. There was a slight breeze because we were higher up on the mountain than Beaverdale. There, Tony's words that he still loved me and wanted me back caressed me like a warm embrace. I was stunned but very much in love with him, so I immediately said yes.

That fall, I started my senior year. I got a job through Vo-Tech where I studied. The Vo-Tech high school program combined academic class-room instruction with on-the-job occupational instruction. So I was able to leave school at noon and get class credit for the work I did at my job. If I wasn't scheduled to work certain days, I was free to go home rather than sitting in study hall all afternoon.

My job was at a grocery store. Since I had to get from school to work, my parents let me drive the Impala. One dark evening when leaving work, I was in a hurry because Tony wanted me to meet him at the lot next to the cemetery before going home. In my haste, I backed into a parked car. I quickly looked around to check if anyone saw what I'd done.

I saw no one. I'd barely tapped the other car's bumper, so I didn't think I'd done any damage. But God was in my head prompting my conscience as the Bible verse says:

"The eyes of the Lord are everywhere, keeping watch on the wicked and the good." (Prov. 15:3)

Getting out of my car, I quickly wrote a note with my name and phone number that explained I'd accidentally backed into the other car's front bumper. I then left to meet Tony. I could only stay fifteen minutes without getting in trouble. We kissed for a little while and made plans for the weekend. Mom was waiting for me the instant I walked in the door.

"Why did it take you so long to drive home? And how did you hit a parked car?"

I looked at her in surprise. She said that a woman called about the note I'd left. She was getting the car inspected by a professional. Two days later, the woman called to say there'd been no real damage other than a slight scrape on the bumper. She didn't want any reimbursement but wanted to express how impressed she was that I'd been responsible enough to leave a note. Mom was impressed too and told me I'd shown real maturity.

I wasn't unaware of the hypocrisy that I would listen to God's voice about hitting a parked car and yet was having a physical relationship out of marriage. Again, I was too blinded by love to let God's voice get through when it came to Tony.

While working at the grocery store on Saturday, I saw an older gentleman fall to the floor. As he reached his hand out toward me, he tried to talk, but he couldn't get the words out. My best guess is that he had a heart attack. Instead of responding, I froze. Trembling violently, I burst into tears.

Someone called an ambulance, but the gentleman had died by the time they arrived. Now, I was crying hysterically. My boss told me I could leave early, and a friend drove me home. I was angry with myself that I'd let the man die without yelling for help or at least walking over and holding his hand. What kind of human being was I?

I will never forget that experience with death. I had no idea if this man had ever placed his faith in Jesus Christ. But I knew for a certainty that I had sinned plenty and deserved to be in hell when I died (Rom. 3:23). In God's great grace and mercy, God had come to this earth in the form of his Son Jesus Christ to die on the cross. He paid the penalty for our sins. Jesus had risen from the dead on the third day, and he was willing to forgive and wipe away the sins of every person who placed their faith in him, offering eternity in heaven with him instead of an eternity in hell. Another way to explain grace is *not* getting what we deserve, which is punishment for our sins. Instead, we get what we *don't* deserve: forgiveness of sin, restoration to God's family as his son or daughter, and eternal life through Jesus Christ our Lord.

I still don't fully understand how our God can be so loving as to forgive me of all the sins and wrong choices for which I'm still struggling to forgive myself. Our God is a loving heavenly Father, and it is by his grace and mercy alone that I am forgiven. As Scripture reminds us, it was God's love that sent his Son Jesus into the world to die a horrible death on a cross to offer us forgiveness through his grace.

"For God so loved the world that he gave his one and only Son, that whoever believes in him shall not perish but have eternal life. For God did not send his Son into the world to condemn the world, but to save the world through him." (John 3:16–17)

My life may not have shown any real faith, but every time I did something wrong, like seeing Tony, guilt consumed me, and I was so grateful for God's grace and mercy. Especially after this horrible experience. That man had died with no warning. If he hadn't already known Jesus as his Savior, he'd had no chance to ask forgiveness and place his faith in Jesus before he died.

And Tony had come so close to dying without warning in that accident. What if something terrible happened to me with no warning? Even though I needed to repent and change the way I was living, I couldn't seem to break Tony's hold and power over me. I worked a few more days at the grocery store, then quit my job.

8. Runaway Wedding

My parents still wouldn't let me see Tony, so I kept sneaking out. He wrecked another car. He'd once again been drinking and fell asleep at the wheel. This didn't affect my devotion. My birthday was fast approaching, so I asked Mom if I could date Tony once I turned eighteen.

"Not as long as you're living under my roof!"

"Fine, then I'll be moving out on my birthday."

My birthday was a whole month before graduation. But I packed my belongings, and Tony picked me up. Mom was horrified. With tears running down her face, she begged me not to leave. As I walked out, not looking back, she called out that she would be praying for me.

I know now Mom was just scared I was making the biggest mistake of my life. She'd married at seventeen to an alcoholic husband, so she knew the struggles I'd face. In the end, she turned out to be correct. But at that point, I was only concerned about being with Tony. I wanted him to love me. I didn't want him to break up with me again. And to make that happen, I needed to be with him.

Tony and I moved into a studio apartment in his parents' apartment building. That weekend, Tony took me to Virginia Beach. In my eighteen years of life, I'd never seen the ocean. Since this was the end of April, the water was frigid, but we went in anyway. Someone took our picture so we'd have a lifetime memory. Tony was making all my dreams come true.

The next day we headed home since I had school on Monday. I finished my last month, and I was surprised but happy when Mom, Jamie, and my paternal grandmother showed up at my graduation. After graduation, I found a job waitressing at a pizzeria just three miles from our apartment. We needed the money since Tony only cleaned cars and did odd jobs for his parents. In addition to my salary, I made good money in tips, so I bought a car to drive back and forth to work. I'd left the Impala behind when I left home.

One night after dinner, Tony handed me an engagement ring with a gorgeous diamond that had belonged to his mother. Since Tony was the oldest of four children, she'd passed the ring on to him. This was a big deal because I felt God would forgive my sinful behavior with Tony if we got married since I'd no longer be living in sin.

I'd come to love my future mother-in-law. She was caring and kind; she never judged me and did her best to give me discreet advice when it came to Tony. I appreciated this because I'd lived with Tony for just a few months when I realized he not only had a serious drinking problem but used way too much marijuana. Since he didn't have a regular job, I began wondering where he was getting his money. The money he made couldn't possibly cover what I saw him spending.

Nor was he being careful with his diabetes. His blood sugar level would get too low because he didn't eat right, and he was constantly having seizures. He liked to go out partying with his friends, and I heard about the numerous fights he got into, which he always won. I assumed that's how he'd earned the nickname Gangster.

My paternal grandmother moved out of her home about this time, and we moved in, planning to buy it. We fixed it up nicely. I was able to quit my waitressing job for a better-paying one in the mailroom at MetLife. By now, Tony and I had been living together for nine months. I'm sure God wasn't happy with me, but I convinced myself he'd forgive me if I married Tony.

We chose our wedding date for May 25th because that was the day we'd first met three years earlier. I asked Mom to help me plan the wedding, thinking this could be a new beginning to heal all the past bad blood between us. Mom, I, and Tony's mom worked to book the church, reception hall, and other elements for the wedding. I was excited when Mom bought my wedding dress.

About this time, Tony started a business. He sold fieldstone, which is the loose rock found naturally on the surface or just below ground. This can be a considerable nuisance for farmers, who must clear it from their fields to plant crops. My grandmother, whose house we lived in, loaned Tony some money to buy a flatbed trailer.

Tony would negotiate with landowners to pick the fieldstone from their land, then load the stone on pallets covered with wire mesh to keep the stone in place. When he had an entire trailer load, he'd sell it to landscapers. I was so proud of all the thought, planning, and hard work he was putting in to build his business.

A month before our wedding, Tony began staying out more and routinely came home drunk. Many times, he didn't come home at all. I loved him with all my heart, but I wondered if this was the kind of life I wanted to live. I couldn't help seeing the similarities between my dad's behavior and what Tony was doing.

I called the wedding off and asked him to move out of the house. He wasn't happy and vowed to win me back. Two weeks later, he asked me out on a date. He was going to church for the first time in his life and hadn't had a drink in two weeks. I was still so angry at God for allowing my dad to get excommunicated and hadn't gone back to church since moving out of my parents' house. But maybe I needed to go with him to church and give Tony a second chance.

Tony moved back into the house. Things went well until his dad ended up in the hospital with lung cancer at the end of May. I was cooking dinner when the ringing of the phone jolted me. His mom said his dad had died. The hum of the lawnmower and the smell of freshly cut grass overwhelmed me as I went outside to tell Tony. He was devastated. His hands shook as he lit a cigarette to calm himself. I didn't know what to say as he wept in my arms, something I'll never forget.

Realizing how fragile life is, Tony's voice was saturated with emotion when he said he wanted me to attend the church he'd found. So we went for the entire next year. But otherwise, my Christian life was almost nonexistent.

A constant inner hollowness haunted me. Would God forget about me permanently? If I didn't do something quickly would I be lost for eternity? At the same time, if I could just love Tony enough for him to truly love me back, the emptiness would go away.

I know now that God was there for me the entire time, patiently waiting for me to turn to him. But God never forces us to follow him. He longs for us to turn to him, but he also gives us free will. My heart had to be ready and willing to seek God before I could find him. God told his people Israel in the Old Testament:

"Then you will call on Me and you will come and pray to Me, and I will hear your voice and I will listen to you. Then with a deep longing you will seek Me and require Me as a vital necessity and you will find Me when you search for Me with all your heart. I will be found by you," says the Lord. (Jer. 29:12–14 [AMP])

Tony and I rescheduled our wedding for the following June, more than a year after our original wedding date. I made Tony agree that we'd move away to start our lives afresh. We moved to Virginia, where Tony had friends. He sold the flatbed trailer and closed out his fieldstone business.

Our wedding day was perfect with beautiful weather. Tony looked so handsome in his white tuxedo. I felt like a princess in the white satin wedding dress and veil Mom had bought for me one year earlier.

"You look so beautiful, sweetheart. I love you."

"I love you too, Mom," I answered, choking up with emotion. "And I want us to have a relationship again. I forgive you for all of the things I've been holding against you for many years. Can you forgive me for my mistakes?"

"Yes, I forgive you too, and I would be so happy to have you back in my life," Mom responded with deep sincerity. I realized then how much she'd always loved me, though, in my immature, hormone-raging adolescence, I'd never been willing to admit it.

After we said our vows, Tony's kiss engulfed me. It branded deep into my skin and beyond. I entirely belonged to him. I would never be alone again.

Tony and I spent our honeymoon in Pennsylvania's gorgeous Pocono Mountains. Our luxury hotel room had a swimming pool, fireplace, hot tub, and a large round bed. Before returning home, we drove to Niagara Falls. The torrent, thunder, and mist of the falls were breathtaking—God's beautiful masterpiece—another experience I'd never forget.

I'd given my two weeks' notice at MetLife. In Virginia, one of Tony's friends let us stay in a spare bedroom until we could save up enough money to rent a place of our own. He also helped Tony get a job as a security guard. Since I'd worked for MetLife in Pennsylvania, I was able to get a job at a local MetLife sales office. After a few months, we finally moved into our own apartment. Everything was going great. If only we could find a church to attend.

I enjoyed my new job and coworkers. By working extra hours, I purchased Tony a special Christmas present—a cruise to the Bahamas. Neither of us had been out of the United States other than Niagara Falls. Our honeymoon had given me a desire to see as much of the world as I could. This seemed like a great way to start. Tony was excited about his Christmas gift. We scheduled the cruise to celebrate our first anniversary in June.

9. Desperate for Love

Although our first Christmas in Virginia was a success, the rest of our marriage was not. Tony insisted on going to Pennsylvania every weekend where we'd stay at his mom's apartment building. Driving several hours each way for a two-night stay after a long week of work was exhausting. I couldn't understand why Tony insisted on doing this, especially since he returned to his prior habits of leaving me alone to party with friends.

One night in Pennsylvania, it was well after midnight and Tony hadn't returned, so I went looking for him. I found him at his favorite bar. He was exceedingly drunk. I pleaded with him to leave with me. He'd borrowed his mom's car, and I didn't want him driving back to the apartment building in that condition.

"Just shut up," Tony growled at me with a lot more unprintable language. When I kept arguing, he backhanded me across the face and knocked me to the floor. In tears, I scrambled to my feet and staggered out the door. Tony eventually made it home without killing himself, and neither of us ever mentioned how he'd struck me.

A few weeks later, I learned why Tony was insisting on all those weekend trips to Pennsylvania. He was transporting marijuana to sell. I didn't know what to do. I quit going with him every weekend and begged him to stop.

His response was to quit being intimate with me. He began telling me I was fat and needed to exercise and get rid of my belly if I wanted him to be attracted to me. I didn't have a belly. At just over five feet, I only weighed a hundred pounds. His constant belittling deeply hurt me, and I wondered if his loss of attraction was why he kept choosing to go to Pennsylvania instead of staying with me.

That wasn't the only way Tony changed. He worked the night shift as a security guard, so he slept during the day. When he woke up, he often appeared to be sleepwalking. He'd urinate in my closet or a corner of our bedroom. I thought he must be getting into much heavier drugs than just marijuana. It got so bad I finally told him he had to quit the drugs or I was going to leave him again. But he swore he wasn't doing drugs.

Neither was he taking care of his diabetes. He liked to go to a nearby buffet and stuff himself with food, which caused his blood sugar to soar so that he had to take extra insulin to get it back down. When this happened, or he ate too much sugar, he became extremely moody. Other times, he made himself sick because he didn't eat when he needed to.

Things got better for a while. June finally came, and we were excited about our cruise to the Bahamas. We flew to Florida and took a taxi to the dock. When we got on the ship, we were amazed that something so enormous could float. The cruise was everything I'd hoped for, and I was delighted that my dream of traveling was finally coming true.

Tony saw an advertisement for parasailing and wanted to try it. I was too afraid of the height but told him I'd be glad to record it on our video camera if he wanted to go. He bought a ticket and headed out on a boat, sailing so high above the water he was just a speck in the sky. I recorded the whole thing.

When he got back on shore, he ran over to me. "Sweetie, Sweetie, guess what I saw?"

"Tell me all about it."

"What do you think I'm trying to do?" he said rather tersely. But he was smiling from cheek to cheek with happiness as he described the enormous manatees he'd seen in the water below him. I loved seeing him so happy. But the very next moment, he spoiled my pleasure. His smile turned to a frown as he looked at my bikini-clad body.

"Put your cover-up on. You look fat like that. People can see your belly."

Crushed, I tugged the cover-up that went with my bikini over my head. I wasn't fat. In fact, I was slim for my height. Why did he keep belittling me?

Tony's health and behavior had been normal during our vacation. But a few weeks into our return, he started getting worse again. Every day he was acting stranger. I assumed he was doing drugs beyond marijuana and once again told him he'd have to choose between me and the drugs. He kept insisting it was just marijuana. He was also once again driving to Pennsylvania every weekend to sell marijuana and get drunk. He told me he missed his friends there. But it seemed clear he just didn't want to be with me.

After several months, I left Tony and headed back to Pennsylvania alone. I quickly found an apartment and two jobs—a full-time factory job and part-time job evenings and weekends at a department store snack counter. Tony seemed devastated that I'd followed through with my many warnings and soon informed me he was moving back to Pennsylvania as well.

My parents hadn't wanted me to marry Tony, but now they were unhappy with me for leaving him. Mom lectured me on how she and Dad had gone through rough patches, especially with his drinking, but that marriage takes perseverance. Clearly she thought I should be fighting harder to make my marriage work. She quoted Genesis 2:24:

"That is why a man leaves his father and mother and is united to his wife, and they become one flesh."

I worked for the next several months. Even with two jobs, I struggled to pay my bills. Meanwhile, Tony didn't have to worry about money since he'd moved back into a spare apartment in his parents' building.

He began stopping by occasionally, trying to talk me into giving him a second chance. Though I still loved him, I didn't want to speak to him. Then one day at my factory job, I had an accident. It wasn't life-threatening, just a piece of metal that pierced my finger while using a machine. But it resulted in a trip to the hospital, where they had to remove the metal, leaving a large, painful hole. I would be off work for several weeks, and the strong pain medicine they gave me meant I couldn't drive home from the hospital. I didn't know what to do, so I called Tony.

He rushed to the hospital and took me home to take care of me. I still loved him so much I decided to give him another chance. After a week together, he told me he'd had to adjust his insulin intake due to working night shifts and sleeping during the day since insulin is administered in different amounts depending on waking and sleeping hours. His doctor, who was in Pennsylvania, hadn't known about his reversed work schedule since he hadn't seen him because we were living in Virginia, so he hadn't adjusted Tony's insulin.

All of which explained Tony's strange behavior. He urged me to call the doctor if I wanted to confirm his story. But I didn't need to as I believed him. Regret ate at me because I'd left him, and it hadn't even been his fault.

We moved back in together. Since his family's apartment building didn't have any apartments with private bathrooms available, we negotiated to rent my parents' home. They had moved into my grandmother's house when we moved to Virginia and rented out their original home.

But I quickly wondered why Tony had even wanted to get back together with me since he again began criticizing my body and rarely so much as kissed or touched me. I was deeply hurt and sure Tony didn't love me anymore. Was Tony seeing other women since he no longer wanted to be intimate with me?

During that same time, my factory job brought me in close contact with a male coworker who was married to the owner of the factory. He was good-looking and flirtatious, telling me I was beautiful and that he sure hoped my husband treated me as well as I deserved.

I laughed off his compliments, but they made me feel warm inside because Tony had become more distant than ever. He stayed late at the bars almost every night, coming home drunk. I'd gained a little weight since our marriage but only weighed 110 pounds, hardly overweight for my height. But he kept telling me I looked fat and needed to go on a diet.

One day at work, I mentioned a new dishwasher someone had given me. Tony had promised to install it but never got around to it. I asked if any of my friends might know someone who could install it. The male coworker said he'd be happy to do it at no charge. Thrilled to get my dishwasher, I arranged for him to come over after work.

He had the dishwasher hooked up in twenty minutes. Tony wasn't there since he'd gone to the bar as usual. Then my coworker began flirting with me and invited me to go out with him. I hesitated since we were both married. But Tony acted as though he couldn't stand to be around me anymore, let alone touch me, and it had been so long since anyone had shown me affection. Meanwhile, this man assured me he was separated from his wife. So I finally agreed to go for a drive the next day after work.

While driving, he told me again that I was beautiful and deserved a man who would truly cherish me. Then he kissed me. It felt so good to be with someone who found me attractive and wanted to be with me. As I had once snuck out of my parents' home to meet Tony, I began sneaking out to meet my coworker and lying to Tony about where I'd been.

Since he was out every night himself, I didn't figure he'd even notice my absence. But one day, I came home to find him in a drunken fit of rage. He slapped me across my face and asked if my boss knew I was seeing her husband. He was acting so violent that I burst into hysterical tears, terrified he'd kill me.

Grabbing the phone, he called my boss's number. When she answered, he screamed at her through slurred words, demanding to know if she was aware her husband was seeing his wife. She eventually got him to put me on the phone. She asked if I was okay and if I needed her to call the police.

She was so nice I felt even worse. I never found out if she knew I'd been seeing her husband, but she didn't deserve what we'd done to her, even if they were separated. I wanted to tell her how sorry I was but didn't want to make things worse.

When I hung up the phone, Tony packed his stuff and left without another word. I never went back to my factory job. Nor did I see my coworker again. I eventually found another full-time job working the night shift at a drug store. A few weeks later, I visited Tony, who'd moved back into his family's apartment building. "Tony, I'm sorry for all the hurtful things I've done." His eyebrows raised as he heard the conciliatory tone in my voice and saw genuine tears of sorrow in my eyes. Pleading for mercy, I begged him to take me back.

His tender response enfolded me in an embrace so genuine I could feel it, "I want you back."

My soul leaked tears. "But, can you forgive me for what I've done?"

In truth, I didn't see how Tony could possibly forgive me when I couldn't forgive myself. What kind of person was I? How could I have done this? Yes,

Tony had treated me abusively and unlovingly. But treating him wrongly in return didn't make anything better.

Bottom line, the whole reason I'd gone out with my coworker was because I wanted so desperately to feel loved again. I was twenty-two years old now and felt as unloved as I had in my teens wishing desperately for my dad's love. This time I'd gone even further over the line searching for love than when I'd snuck out to be with Troy and Tony. I needed to ask God's forgiveness as what I'd done was a huge sin. But now, I was convinced I was so far off God's radar that he'd never hear my prayer even if I tried to talk to him. A verse I'd learned filled my memory and my heart. Scripture pounded furiously at my mind:

"What benefit did you reap at that time from the things you are now ashamed of? Those things result in death!" (Rom. 6:21)

Was it too late for me? Could I expect any future but the punishment I knew I deserved—eternal separation from God?

10. Joni

Though I couldn't forgive myself, Tony insisted he still loved me and wanted to come home. Things went okay for the next year other than Tony's continued partying every weekend, drinking, and marijuana use and sales, not to mention wrecking additional cars while under the influence. I wasn't happy about any of this or even sure I still loved Tony, much less that he loved me. But because of my own wrongdoing I believed I owed it to him to put up with his behavior.

By this time, Tony and I had moved to Ohio so Tony could help his cousin Larry start a business. Larry seemed nice and I hoped he might be a good influence on Tony. Tony and I also started attending church again.

I hadn't found a job yet. While unpacking, I'd come across a Bible Mom insisted on giving me when I moved out. Though I'd kept it, I'd forgotten all about it. Bored sitting at home all day, I began reading it. To my surprise, I couldn't put it down and read the entire Bible in one month.

Attending church with Tony and reading the Bible gave me hope this Ohio move could be a new beginning for our marriage. Maybe together we could learn how to be better people and live our lives the way God intended for us to live them. I read the description of faith in the New Testament epistle to the Hebrews:

"Now faith is confidence in what we hope for and assurance about what we do not see... And without faith it is impossible to please God, because anyone who comes to him must believe that he exists and that he rewards those who earnestly seek him." (Heb. 11:1, 6)

Please, God, give me the faith to do this. I prayed desperately. *I know it's impossible to please you without faith.*

That next month, I landed a great job at an insurance company, New York Life. During training, they gave us an aptitude test to determine how much we knew about life insurance. Thanks to my last two jobs with MetLife, I received a perfect score.

Out of thirty new hires, one would become a senior underwriter, three junior underwriters, and the rest would have clerical positions. I was thrilled to be selected for the senior underwriter position. This not only meant a much higher salary than I'd had at MetLife but substantial raises in the future as I proved myself.

Tony was happy I'd gotten an excellent job. But he still constantly yelled at me for being unattractively fat and refused to be intimate with me. He told me I needed to exercise more to be as skinny as when he'd met me. Sure, I was ten pounds heavier at twenty-three than at sixteen, but my body was also different as a grown woman, and by no normal standards was I overweight. Why was he so cruel?

We were only in Ohio six months when Tony found some investors to start his fieldstone business again. I hated leaving my new job, especially since my salary was far higher than Tony had ever earned with his business. But I believed God would want me to make my marriage a top priority, even if that meant sacrifices. So I resigned from New York Life, and we moved back to Pennsylvania, renting a two-bedroom apartment in his mother's building.

For the first months back, I was able to get unemployment benefits since I'd had to quit my job to move with my husband. This provided enough income to live on until Tony could get his business started and I could find another job. Tony was now home most weekday evenings working on paperwork. But he was again gone all day and out partying every weekend.

I suggested returning to the church we'd attended when we were newlyweds, but he had no interest. Since I didn't want to go by myself, I quit attending church too. Tony was constantly drunk. He wrecked several more cars falling asleep at the wheel. By now, I'd lost count. At least he typically only spent a few hundred dollars for each car, junking them once he destroyed them.

I began getting phone calls out of nowhere while Tony was at work, sometimes several times a day. When I answered, the caller would hang up. When I told Tony, he said not to worry. Then one day, Tony's friend Jim came to town. That evening, they went out partying. Bored with sitting at home, I wanted to go along, but Tony said no.

When I awoke at 5:00 a.m., Tony still wasn't home. I could hear Jim in his room, so they must have come home at some point. But where was Tony? I looked outside, but Tony's car wasn't there. Knocking on Jim's door, I asked if he knew where Tony was.

"Oh, he went back out after dropping me off."

Stunned, I hurried back to my bedroom and got dressed. Grabbing my purse and keys, I went looking for Tony. I drove to the bar where he usually hung out. As I expected, it was closed. I continued driving around the block. I spotted Tony's car parked outside an apartment building. That made no sense, so I parked across the street and waited.

It was daylight before Tony emerged from the apartment building. A young, pretty girl with long brown hair stood behind him in the doorway. Tony kissed her before heading to his car. Shocked, I didn't even try to confront him but rushed home.

I made it into the apartment only a few minutes before Tony entered. Throwing my clothes off, I climbed back into bed and pretended to be asleep. Tears streamed down my face, and I could only hope Tony wouldn't notice my body shaking as I stifled my sobs.

The following day, Tony went out again. By midnight, he was still not home. Driving to the apartment where I'd seen Tony and the brown-haired girl, I knocked on the front door, waited, then knocked again. After several minutes of knocking, I decided everyone was too soundly asleep to hear my pounding or no one was home.

I drove back home and went to bed. Several hours later, Tony still hadn't returned. Getting out of bed, I drove back to the apartment building. I parked next to Tony's car. I walked up the steps, shaking with nerves. But I was also determined. I pounded on the door as loudly as I could.

A few minutes later, the brown-haired girl opened the door. I realized she was just a child, no older than sixteen, the age I'd been when I met Tony.

"What's your name?" I demanded.

She looked at me strangely. "Joni. What do you want?"

Instead of answering, I pushed past her into the apartment, shouting, "Where is he? Tony! Tony, where are you?"

Tony emerged into the kitchen, his face white from shock. I stared at him in disbelief, then demanded, "Do you want her?"

"Yes," he responded to my shock.

I looked at the girl. "Do you want him?"

"Yes," she mumbled.

What was Tony thinking being with this child half his age? It only occurred to me sometime later that he'd targeted Joni for the same reason he'd once targeted me. Though he was now in his thirties, he clearly preferred young, immature, not fully developed teens to an "old, fat" 110-pound, fully adult woman of twenty-three.

My heart pounded so hard it hurt, and I wanted to attack them both. But though I was estranged from God, I had peace in the midst of a raging storm. Through a turbulent tsunami of emotion, I somehow heard a voice inside my head telling me not to fight but to let God win this battle. Looking from one to the other, I simply said, "You two deserve each other. Have a nice life."

Storming out of the apartment, I slammed the door behind me. I had no idea why I'd chosen not to fight, and I hate to think of what might have happened if I'd given in to my furious impulses. I know now it was the Holy Spirit helping me to walk away. My shaking legs made it difficult to press the accelerator as my car jerkily sped down the road.

When I got home, I climbed back into bed. A half hour later, footsteps echoed through the apartment. While Tony climbed into bed, I asked him if he was at least going to apologize. Looking me straight in the eye, he sneered, "You cheated on me once. I pay you back threefold."

I was again stunned. After all, Tony was the one who'd initially forced me to accept other men's kisses. Yes, I'd cheated on him once, but he'd been cheating on me since we'd first dated. And not just the times I knew about. I recognized now what I'd tried to shut my eyes to these past several years.

What kind of man stays out all night drinking and isn't cheating on his wife? Especially when he refuses intimacy with her. Even my alcoholic dad came home to his wife before midnight.

I wanted to leave him, but I kept telling myself he was right and that I deserved his abusive treatment after my own transgression. I told him he had to choose between Joni and me. He finally said he chose me and wouldn't see Joni anymore. But I no longer had any faith that he was speaking the truth.

I came to realize that no matter how many times he'd cheated on me and how much he protested he still loved me, part of him hated me for having cheated on him that one time. He'd never trust me again, and I would never be able to trust him either, however young, naïve, and foolish I'd been to trust him in the first place.

11. The Best Gift

One month later, I was reading a book when the ringing of the phone startled me out of my reverie. The caller hung up when I answered. Not again. With the old adage in mind, "keep your friends close and your enemies closer," I went to visit Joni. My trembling legs barely made it up the steps to the door. I knocked. My throat tightened as footsteps came closer to the door. My pulse raced as the lock turned. When the handle turned, I stood there frozen, unsure of what to do. My brain urged me to run, but my nerves paralyzed me. My feet were cemented in place as I faced the beautiful girl. After her initial shock when she realized who I was, she asked, "What do *you* want?"

"I need to talk to you about Tony. I am his wife." I showed her my wedding ring. She hesitated. Then she invited me into the apartment. I looked around the kitchen. There were tons of dirty dishes piled on the counters by the sink and a lot of papers on the table. I saw some mail on the table and noticed two names on the envelopes.

"Let's sit in the living room because my son is watching TV." As I walked through the hallway, the old flooring creaked. I was trying not to step on anything, but it was impossible. I stepped on kids' toys that were all over the floor. The stained, suspended ceiling looked like it was about to fall, and the carpet wasn't much better, that is, what I could see of it. The TV was so loud I could barely hear Joni when she yelled, "Well, start talking."

After she turned down the TV, I looked into Joni's tear-filled eyes and pleaded with her to tell me if she was still seeing my husband. Reluctantly she talked to me. She was a nice person and didn't deserve to get mixed up with the likes of Tony. Despite her young age, she already had a two-year-old son. She was struggling financially and clearly falling head over heels for Tony.

I couldn't blame her for that. Tony knew how to make a girl feel like the most loved person in the world. That's what he did with me. He got into my mind and made me feel like no one else could love me the way he did. Joni saw a smooth talker with his own business who flashed around so much money that people assumed he was rich.

That was far from the truth. Tony's business paid him minimum wage for six months out of the year. Selling marijuana was where he made his money. Tony can outlie the best con man. He'd told Joni he wasn't married. She'd thought I was a jealous ex-girlfriend. I found out Tony had never stopped seeing her. Joni and I decided that he'd have to choose between us. It wasn't fair for him to have us both.

When I told Tony, he was so angry that I thought he might kill me. I didn't hear from Joni for about a month when she called and said her toilet wasn't working. She wondered if Tony would come and fix it. I immediately went to her apartment and fixed her toilet. We hung out a few more times after that. Tony finally got the picture that he wouldn't be able to keep secrets from us and quit seeing her.

A few months later, I was hired again at MetLife, thanks to a great recommendation from my previous boss in Virginia. The new job was full-time with vacation, health, dental, and vision benefits. Meanwhile, Tony kept building his business. He even got government funding by hiring prisoners. He had to buy a van to transport the prisoners, but the government paid most of their wages. I was proud of Tony for his business success even though he occasionally borrowed my credit cards when things went wrong and he needed a bailout.

One weekend, while on vacation in Virginia, we toured a time-share. The salesman, Joe, met us outside the condo. The tall man's face was flushed as he walked up to Tony. He extended his hand. Tony looked him right in the eye and his large calloused hand gripped Joe's with a firm shake. I fell in love with the condo. Tony said it wasn't good enough and asked if he had anything more luxurious. Joe whispered to Tony and I followed the men to the car.

After driving for five minutes through trees on a very curvy mountain road, we parked in front of another condo. Joe and Tony were talking to me, but I didn't hear them because I was enamored with the summit of the ski lift. Inside there were two skylights, a fireplace, and a whirlpool tub. My husband always insisted on the best of everything. I insisted on buying it and the salesman beamed. I read Tony's serious facial expression, compared to his normal jovial one. I knew instantly to shut my mouth. He negotiated the deal with Joe and we only paid a little more than the entry-level condo price. It was the best decision I'd made. My dream of traveling would begin to come true because of that decision. Tony was pleased with his skills and happy about our purchase too.

That spring, I approached my parents about purchasing their Beaverdale house so Tony and I could have a place of our own. Since they were collecting rental income, they'd be reluctant to sell. Eventually, they agreed to let us buy it because they loved me. We installed carpeting, repainted everything, and remodeled the bathroom.

That following April, Tony asked me what I wanted for my twenty-sixth birthday. I asked him to make love to me since he never touched me anymore. Though I was fairly certain Joni was out of the picture, I knew subconsciously he must have another girlfriend because he was not one to go without sex. I needed to do something to save my marriage and make him love me again.

Tony surprised me with a memorable birthday, complete with a candlelight dinner and a beautiful gold-plated bracelet. He had the words "I love you" along with my name engraved on the bracelet.

A few weeks later, I realized my period was overdue. An over-the-counter pregnancy test confirmed I was pregnant. I didn't want to tell Tony until I was sure. A doctor's appointment confirmed I was about six weeks along. That meant I'd gotten pregnant on my birthday since that was the only time Tony and I had been intimate in months. A baby was the best gift Tony had ever given me.

I could hardly wait to tell him. Rushing home, I prepared a special candlelight dinner and bought flowers just like Tony had done for my birthday. The house couldn't have smelled more like flowers if we were in a garden. I styled my hair, put on a pretty outfit, and waited for him to come home from work.

When he finally got home, I could tell he'd been drinking, so maybe he hadn't been at work after all. I told him I was pregnant. I'll never forget the look on his face as he stared me straight in the eyes and asked, "Who's the father? Because it sure as heck isn't me!"

Stunned, I burst into tears, wailing, "What do you mean? Of course, you're the father!"

He turned around and walked out the door. I was devastated when he didn't come home that night. I eventually cried myself to sleep on the couch. When he finally came home the next day, with tears rolling down his face, he asked, "Are you telling the truth? Is this really my baby?"

"Who else's baby do you think it could be?" I whispered. Then he embraced me, kissing away the dark circles under my eyes. I told him the due date in January, forty weeks after my birthday when we'd made love. He was ecstatic.

Over the next several months, I worked as much overtime as possible so I could take a six-month leave of absence after our baby was born. I worked fourteen-hour days Monday through Friday and twelve-hour days on Saturdays. The overtime allowed me to stash away a fair amount of savings and pay ahead on the house loan. I worked until December when my doctor told me I should stop.

Tony refused to be intimate with me the whole time I was pregnant. He kept telling me I was too fat and ugly. I was increasingly depressed because I thought he didn't love me anymore. But with my pregnancy weight gain, I too felt fat and ugly, so I didn't argue.

We decided on two names for the baby, Lacey or Luke Jacob. I decorated our second bedroom in a mint-green color suitable for either a boy or a girl in preparation for our baby. My mom and sister-in-law Debbie threw me a baby shower. I received a crib and everything I needed.

Tony wouldn't go to doctor appointments with me. He was never home and didn't seem to care much about me. I became concerned he wouldn't show up for our baby's birth, and I was increasingly scared of dying in childbirth. As a Christian, even if not an extremely committed one, I had the assurance I'd go to heaven if I died. But I desperately wanted to raise my child. I knew Tony wasn't capable of raising a child since he couldn't even take care of himself with his drinking.

On January 16, I started having sharp pains, but they weren't true contractions. It was false labor. I was so uncomfortable I couldn't sleep. I wanted this baby to come.

Just over a week later, Luke or Lacey began coming with or without Tony. I called Mom. She was on her way over when Tony showed up. We headed to the hospital, a fifty-minute drive. I was admitted, but after several hours nothing further happened. Tony returned to Beaverdale, then came back, then left again. I was worried he wouldn't be there for the birth, but there was nothing I could do about it. At least Mom was with me. That would have to be enough.

The next day at 1:36 p.m., the twenty-fourth of January, Tony arrived just in time. After over thirty hours of labor, Luke Jacob Yuzwa was born. He was eight pounds, three ounces, and nineteen and three-quarter inches long. Luke's brown hair matched Tony's contrasting against his smooth bone china skin. Tony beamed. He took turns with Mom holding Luke before I took my baby back.

Tony left. I learned later he was so excited he'd told everyone he was a dad. The lady at the post office. The people at the gas station. His family. And of course, everyone at the bar.

The hospital photographer took pictures of Luke. We'd bought a beautiful mint-green outfit since we hadn't known whether to expect a boy or girl. It fit perfectly. The following day, Luke and I were released, and Tony drove us home.

Luke's birth was a major turning point in my life. My son was the greatest gift I'd been given, and the Bible tells us:

"Every good and perfect gift is from above, coming down from the Father of the heavenly lights, who does not change like shifting shadows." (James 1:17)

My most important job was to make sure my son knew Jesus. Mom still attended the same church where I grew up, so every Sunday we went with her. Tony refused to go with me, but this time I didn't let that discourage me.

After church, I'd take Luke to my parents' house. Mom would cook Sunday dinner, and we'd visit for a few hours. Sometimes Dad was even there.

I recognized it would take a few years before Luke was old enough to understand much about God. But I didn't want him turning out like me. I'd walked so far away from my heavenly Father and my faith over the last several years. Now it was time to make things right. I wanted to dedicate the rest of my life and the raising of my child to God.

12. Loving Dad

Tony loved being a father. He'd hold Luke for hours, singing songs he made up: "Little Luke, he's my boy, makes me happy, full of joy."

For Valentine's Day, Tony bought me two dozen roses and a ring with five diamonds.

Although he dearly loved his son, he soon returned to his prior attitude toward me. Tony resumed complaining about how fat I looked. I took care of Luke, cleaned the house, and cooked while Tony ran around all day with his friends. I got up several times a night with Luke, which was exhausting. But Tony made clear any care for Luke was my job.

In March, I came across some inexpensive tickets to Cancun in a travel magazine. I yearned to travel more, and this looked like a wonderful vacation we could take in the summer. When I suggested the trip to Tony, he reminded me that his fieldstone business would be starting back up. But he suggested I go with my sister. He agreed to care for Luke, who would be five months old by then, so I could have a carefree time with my sister.

Maybe I was impulsive and selfish leaving Luke at such a young age. I'd never been a mother before. But between my mom and a Christian family from Mom's church, I'd arranged babysitters for Luke during the day. I had confidence Tony was up to caring for him at night. He'd demonstrated how much he loved his son and enjoyed being with him. After all, it would just be a few days. My sister agreed it was a fantastic idea, so we booked our tickets for June.

On Mother's Day, Tony gave me two presents. One was from Luke—a three-inch mirror topped with the word Mom in beautiful glass calligraphy. I loved it. Then Tony gave me his gift. Opening the red-velvet box, I found inside a unique ring. Tony had designed it himself. It was gold and Z-shaped with two stones, my birthstone, a diamond since I was born in April, and a beautiful red garnet, Luke's birthstone.

Tony explained this was called a mother's ring. Overcome with emotion, I burst into happy tears. Giving him a tight hug, I thanked him over and over. This was one gift I would treasure forever.

The day finally came for Jamie and me to fly to Cancun. Once there, we booked a boat excursion, did a jungle tour, and took a turn on a Jet Ski. I bought Tony a classy marble chess set. He liked playing chess with me, but I always lost since I never understood all the rules.

That night, I called Tony to see how he and Luke were doing. He said everything was good. I reminded Tony he needed to eat every meal so his blood sugar didn't get out of control. I also begged him not to drink. He promised he wouldn't. I told him that I loved him and would call the following evening.

The next day, Jamie and I took a bus trip to the Mayan ruins of Chichen Itza. At one point, several men stopped the bus and got on, brandishing machine guns. One man walked down the aisle, pointing a machine gun at each person as he went past. They finally left. I think the bus driver must have paid them off.

I still have no idea what they were looking for. Jamie was terrified, but I guess I was too ignorant to be scared, probably for the best in that situation. As with marrying Tony, it was one more indication that I had no real common sense or street smarts.

The flight home seemed to take forever. I was missing my baby boy. I'd been away for five days, and I had to trust that Tony had kept his promise not to get inebriated while Luke was in his care. I'd called every night, and everything sounded fine.

Sure enough, all seemed fine when I arrived home. Luke was healthy and happy and excited to see his mama. Tony said he'd enjoyed spending time with him. Between Mom and the church family babysitting, he'd been able to work every day. He'd even occasionally taken Luke with him when he had to drive around to do errands.

But within a few days of my return, Tony was back to going out drinking in the evenings. I hoped he'd kept his promise while I was away, and thankfully, everything had turned out all right. But I realized that the next time I had an impulsive brainstorm, I needed to put my son first.

Tony always came home before Luke's bedtime to kiss him goodnight. But then he'd immediately go back out. I tried to talk him out of going, warning that one of these days when he had another wreck, he wouldn't be so lucky. I knew Luke meant more to him than anything else in this world, so why would he want to risk not being a part of that?

In July, I booked a trip to Myrtle Beach, South Carolina. Since Tony was busy with work, only my mom, Luke, and I went. It was the first time Luke had been to the ocean. Mom and I took turns dipping his feet in the surf, but the cold water made him cry. At this age, he didn't love the beach as much as I did. We drove inland to visit my maternal grandmother, who'd never seen Luke. Mom was excited since she didn't get to see her mother often.

The summer went by fast with Luke growing bigger every day. He was very much Daddy's little boy. When Tony came home each day from work, Luke's face lit up and he'd reach his hands out for Tony to pick him up. Tony would toss him up in the air over and over while Luke laughed and laughed. I envied their bond. I dearly loved my son, but Tony and Luke loved each other in an extraordinary way. Tony would sit on the porch in the sunshine smoking cigarettes and talking to Luke for hours on end.

My maternity leave ended just after Labor Day. I hated going back to work at MetLife, but my job was our main income. Our health and dental coverage was also through my job, so I reluctantly went back. Mom's church friends agreed to babysit Luke while I was at work. Tony would drop Luke off each morning, and I'd pick him up after work.

I'd been back to work only a few weeks when Tony called me at work to say his blood sugar level was low and I needed to come home. My babysitters couldn't watch Luke that day, so he was with Tony, who wasn't working. Before Luke's birth, I'd have tried calling someone in his family for help. Now I immediately told my boss I had an emergency and had to leave.

Rushing home, I found Tony on the floor having a diabetic seizure. I called an ambulance. Luke was sitting on the floor nearby, eating paper. Tony was fine once they got his blood sugar level under control. But the image of my baby boy sitting there helpless next to his convulsing father was ingrained in my brain and would never leave me.

In October, Tony and Luke were playing while I made dinner. Tony suddenly called me into the living room. I found Luke standing up with one hand holding onto the couch, trying to take his first step toward Tony. He was in shorts and a T-shirt since our house got fairly hot from the coal heat. I grabbed the camera and snapped a picture of father and son together, Luke standing on his chubby legs, giggling with joy, while Tony smiled from ear to ear, eyes bright with his love for Luke. What a great day.

13. A New Home

With Luke awake a good bit of the night, I tried to sleep in as long as possible until Luke woke up. But Luke shared a bedroom with Tony's business office, including the phone and answering machine. Many days, Luke and I were startled awake by the ringing of the office phone. We needed to do something about it, but the house wasn't big enough to move the office. We looked for a bigger house in our area that fit our budget.

One day, Tony found a house for sale in Dunlo, a small unincorporated community a short distance from Beaverdale. He knew the owner and believed he could make a deal. The house needed some work to be livable, but it had a big kitchen, living room, dining room, laundry room, bathroom, and three bedrooms. We agreed on a sale price, signed all the paperwork, applied for a loan, and soon closed on the house.

We started the necessary remodeling so we could move in as soon as possible. I'd bought a whirlpool tub for the upstairs bathroom, so one day, I stopped by the house to check how Tony was doing with the installation. I smelled something strange but didn't see anything that could be causing it. I opened a door leading from the bathroom into a twelve-foot by twenty-six-foot walk-in attic. Marijuana plants hung from every rafter. The smell was overwhelming.

Freaking out, I yelled, "Tony, get your butt up here, now!"

I'd known he was driving to Ohio to buy marijuana, which he then brought back to Pennsylvania to sell. I also knew I couldn't stop him from using it or selling it. I'd tried to convince Tony of the severe ramifications of his illegal activities, both to himself and our family, but he simply didn't care. Still, bringing it into our home and around our infant son was another matter.

When Tony walked into the attic, he looked at my beet red face and knew he was in trouble. I bellowed, "Clear the marijuana out of the house, and if you ever bring drugs into our home again, you'll never see Luke or me again."

"If you try to take Luke away from me, you'll be the one who never sees your son again." I felt as though my head exploded and I couldn't piece together my fragmented thoughts. Should I dare to leave Tony?

The Holy Spirit had been convicting me lately, especially during church, and in the core of my heart, I believed God was judging me for living with a man who could do all these bad things. But I couldn't leave Tony, and I hadn't had the courage to leave him before Luke was born. If I left him now, I had no doubt he'd carry out his threat and I'd never see Luke again.

I eventually found out that Tony had grown a whole field of marijuana. I was stunned and furious because I was working my butt off at my job, paying all the bills and health insurance. Tony was only contributing the minimum earnings from his fieldstone business while raking in money from drug sales.

It took a few months to finish work on the house, so we spent Luke's first Christmas in the Beaverdale house. Luke received many presents, but at eleven months old, he was far more interested in playing with the wrapping paper and gift boxes.

After moving into our new home at the beginning of January, Luke said his first word—Dada. Lucky Tony. I might have physically given birth to Luke, and I knew he loved his mommy, but father and son were inseparable with an unbreakable bond I could only dream of.

Meanwhile, Tony was still drinking every evening and constantly using marijuana. Luke's first birthday was January 24, but it was an icy, snowy day in February when we finally held his party. I ordered pizza from a local pizza shop and a cake from our local grocery store, and everyone we invited showed up.

We sang happy birthday and Luke blew out the candles. After each bite of cake, Luke made me wipe his hands off. I'll never forget that he liked to be neat like his mother. That was a precious moment.

In March, Luke said his first sentence: "I love you." Tony and I were in the room and very excited. Tony was holding Luke, so the words were probably meant for him. Though still drinking almost every evening, Tony came home each night to say goodnight to Luke before his bedtime.

In the past year, Tony had again wrecked at least two more cars and got a DUI. This resulted in losing his license and several hefty fines. He didn't care and kept driving without a license.

His diabetes was also out of control. He'd call me at work at least once a week, telling me he had a low blood sugar level. I said I couldn't keep leaving work every time he called. He needed to start eating more regularly instead of waiting until his blood sugar level got low and then trying to figure out what to eat.

Even worse, he often had Luke with him when this happened. He'd go into a seizure and leave his one-year-old son to take care of himself. I had to call Tony's Aunt Lorraine several times to take care of them until I could leave work. Or I'd call my elderly neighbor Phyllis to cook him eggs or a grilled cheese sandwich. I didn't know what else to do. Why a grown man couldn't take care of himself was beyond me.

I wanted to quit my job so I could take care of my son. But we needed my income, and we definitely needed the health insurance my job provided for all the times we had to take Tony to the hospital or call an ambulance for him. I arranged for Luke to go to the babysitter every day I worked. But I had to leave the house quite early, which meant Luke had to stay with Tony until the babysitter was available. If I quit my job, we'd lose our home and car since Tony drank away his measly salary, and our household never saw a penny from his marijuana sales.

One day when I was at work, Tony called me around 9:00 a.m. to say that Luke had a rash all over him. I didn't know how to respond other than to ask if he'd called the doctor and made an appointment.

"Does Luke seem to be feeling okay?"

"Yes, he doesn't act like anything's wrong. He's playing and watching TV."

That hardly sounded like an emergency, so I finished my day at work. When I got home and saw Luke, I gasped in horror. His skin was red all over as though he'd been scalded.

"Why didn't you tell me?" I yelled at Tony.

He shrugged. "I did."

"You didn't tell me it was this bad. I'd have left work if I'd known how bad it really was," I cried hysterically. That upset Luke. But I was truly terrified, so we rushed him to the doctor. They diagnosed the rash as hives and gave us an antihistamine to treat it, but it took several weeks for the rash to go away.

By now, I was desperate to repair my broken marriage. At the beginning of April, I begged Tony to go to Cape Cod, Massachusetts, with me. My paternal grandmother offered to keep Luke for the week so Tony and I could spend some quality time together. I was so excited when Tony agreed to go.

Our first stop was Newport, Rhode Island, a ten-hour drive. We dropped Luke off and drove all night, arriving at the time-share I'd booked early in the morning. To my disappointment, Tony got high before and during the trip.

My plans included deep-sea fishing, seeing Plymouth Rock, and touring the Newport Mansions. We spent the first day fishing. The ocean was pretty rough, but I caught a relatively large shark within fifteen minutes of putting my line in the water. My next catch was a wolffish with sharp canine teeth. Tony recorded everything. Then I caught another shark followed by a fairly large cod. All but the cod were released back into the water.

Meanwhile to his chagrin, Tony had not caught a single fish. We went back to our time-share where we enjoyed a delicious dinner. I called my grandmother to talk to Luke, a mostly one-sided conversation, then went to bed.

That was the end of spending quality time as a couple. I completed the rest of our planned itinerary by myself. Tony claimed he had to make business calls. But when I got back from sightseeing each evening, I'd find him at the bar or in the pool talking to girls. I could tell he'd been drinking and using marijuana. So much for repairing our marriage. I couldn't fix it by myself.

Five days into our trip, Tony said he wanted to leave even though we had the time-share through the end of the week. He said that he missed Luke. So we drove all through the night back to Pennsylvania.

Near the middle of April, Tony said he wanted to talk. He asked if Luke and I would be okay if anything were to happen to him.

"We'll be fine. But you don't need to talk like that because nothing is going to happen to you."

I assured him that I couldn't imagine life without him and that Luke needed his daddy. Tony loved Luke, and I didn't think he would want to leave us, especially Luke. So I was confused why we were having this conversation.

When my birthday came in April, Tony surprised me with roses, a card, and tickets to the World Wrestling Federation.

Later that week, I put my foot down again with Tony. "You need to quit using drugs, and you need to take care of yourself. Since you don't work, you are taking care of Luke. With your self-destructive behavior again out of control, I fear for our son's life. I will leave you if you continue using drugs, and I will fight you in court to get custody of our son."

I knew Tony would never actually let me out the door with Luke, but to my surprise, he agreed to go to marriage counseling with me. The very next day, we attended our first session. The counselor spoke to us individually. Then he spoke with us as a couple.

When we left, we scheduled our next counseling appointment. Little did we know we would never keep that appointment.

14. THE WORST DAY

On May 14, 1999, Tony came home to say goodnight to Luke after I'd already put him to bed. I could tell he'd been drinking. He asked where Luke was.

"He's asleep. You're late. It's already past his bedtime."

"That's ridiculous," Tony ranted, then headed toward the door. Worried about him driving drunk, I begged him to stay home.

"Mind your own business and stop telling me what to do," he yelled.

In a last-ditch effort to keep Tony from leaving, I called after him, "You know you're going to wreck. If you leave this house, you're going to die!"

His eyes shot daggers at me as he bolted out. I don't know what came over me to say those words. I was at my wit's end. Whether his drinking, the marijuana, or diabetes, every day was a battle. I loved Tony with all my heart, but I hated watching him destroy himself.

The doorbell woke me around 6:00 a.m. Since Tony wasn't in bed, I assumed he'd come home drunk and couldn't unlock the door. To my surprise, two police officers stood outside.

"Are you Tammy Yuzwa, wife of Anthony Yuzwa?"

"Yes, I am. What did he do?"

Instead of answering, the officers asked to come in. The officer told me to take a seat. Then one of the officers said, "We are sorry to inform you, but your husband has been in an accident. It happened at 4:00 a.m."

Since this was far from the first time, my first thought wasn't for Tony. "Was anyone else hurt? I told Tony just last night he was going to wreck again if he insisted on driving."

"It doesn't appear anyone else was in the vehicle." Then the words I'll never forget: "It gets worse. He died when the car caught on fire. He was burned beyond recognition, so you won't be able to have a viewing."

Blinking back stinging tears, waves of despair crashed and pounded in my mind. "Are you sure it's him?"

"We've confirmed the identity as your husband."

Tears sprang unchecked to my eyes. "I want to see him. I've *got* to see him."

"Ma'am, that won't be possible," the officer stated, too matter-of-factly. "In fact, we strongly suggest he be cremated immediately. We will be in touch with more details later. Can you call someone to be with you?"

I was trembling from head to toe as I called my mom. "Mom, Tony's gone. He was in an accident." I kept repeating this over and over.

Tony was only thirty-six years old when he died. At twenty-eight years old, I was now a widow and a single mother. Despite all his faults, Tony had been my world since I was sixteen, and I was both worried about my future and terrified of raising Luke on my own. How would God get me through this? He was my only hope.

Mom arrived not long after the officers left, and we fell into each other's arms, weeping. Mom stayed by my side as I undertook the terrible task of calling Tony's family.

I was so grateful to have Mom back in my life. I couldn't imagine dealing with all of this without her. I told her how drunk Tony had been and that I'd begged him not to go out. I wished I'd fought harder to keep him from going out and that I'd told him I loved him. That I'd done my best to warn him was of little comfort now. Why couldn't we at least have been able to say goodbye? And how was I going to explain this to our one-year-old son?

I went into Luke's room to see if he was awake, surprised the doorbell hadn't awakened him when the police came. He normally cried for me to come and get him when he woke up. He was sitting in his crib, murmuring. I picked him up. Hugging him tightly, I told him that his daddy had gone away and wouldn't be able to see him anymore. I tried to stop crying. I wanted to be strong for Luke, but I couldn't.

The coroner called later to say that he ruled Tony's death as a motor vehicle accident. They'd had to identify him by his dental records because his burns made him unrecognizable. The accident had initially been called in as a brush fire. When fire crews arrived on the scene, they'd realized a car was involved but didn't discover someone was inside until they'd put out the fire.

Tony's blood-alcohol level was more than twice the legal limit. The car had struck a guard rail, gone off the other side of the road, and hit a tree. The impact had caused the fire. There were no signs he'd tried to brake. I explained how he'd fallen asleep driving before, causing multiple crashes.

Tony's funeral was two days later. I planned to scatter Tony's ashes in the ocean. Tony's best friend told me Tony had quit taking his insulin a short time before his death. He'd always complained about having to give himself shots twice a day. I couldn't understand why he made it such a big deal. Painful memories flashed through my mind like an angry flash flood. Stress assaulted me like the ocean's tides, threatening to pull me into the abyss.

At that moment, the pieces suddenly clicked in my mind. Tony asking me whether Luke and I would be okay if something happened to him. Quitting his insulin. The reckless behavior and drinking. I don't think he intentionally set out to kill himself that night, but he'd definitely given up on life. He'd known he was on an inevitable pathway to death, whether in a car accident, another seizure, or diabetic coma from a high or low insulin level. The need to know why Tony wanted to end it all sucked me in like a powerful riptide pulling me away from the safety of the shore.

Why would Tony give up on life when he loved his son more than anything? Another of his friends told me that Tony was afraid he'd end up being a bad father and ruining Luke's life. In the end, Tony's death would end up hurting Luke as much or more than his life could have by leaving a gaping emotional hole. Luke would grow up trying to emulate his father to feel close to him, and that would eventually ruin Luke's life and mine too.

After the funeral, I tried to go back to work at MetLife, but I couldn't do it. I sat at my desk and wept. I still had Tony's stone business, so I decided to quit my job and concentrate on running the business and raising Luke. Once

I took over sales calls, I was able to sell several loads of stone, which helped with the bills. I also paid off the Beaverdale and Dunlo houses with Tony's life insurance.

Occasionally, I took Luke to the babysitter to give myself more time with the business. Other times, I took him with me on the front-end loader to pick up rocks. Luke loved this, but I was cautious about doing it often as the work could be dangerous and there were snakes in the woods. Some of my workers were bitten and had to go to the hospital.

I heard Tony's voice every time someone called and left a message on the business answering machine. I couldn't bring myself to replace it. Miserable as my marriage had been, I still deeply loved Tony and grieved that he was gone.

My parents came to visit us frequently. Even though Dad was still drinking, it seemed Tony's death had positively impacted him, making him realize how important family is. Sometimes he'd even call and ask me to bring Luke over for a visit. We were already there every Sunday to attend church with Mom. We went to their house for lunch. Unlike in the past, Dad would intentionally make sure he was home while we were there. Mom also babysat Luke when needed and loved spending time with her first grandson.

Luke, in turn, dearly loved his grandparents. On one occasion when they were visiting, Luke was so upset about them leaving they had to sneak out the kitchen door. When he discovered they'd left, he went ballistic. He screamed and cried for them for an hour. I wondered if maybe he was worried he'd never see them again as happened with his dad. In the evenings, if he heard a car door shut somewhere outside, he'd run to the door yelling, "Dada."

That broke my heart. I explained through tears that Dada wasn't coming home anymore. Luke was still too young to understand death, heaven and hell, or life after death. I had no way of knowing what Tony's heart toward God had been at the moment he died, but I knew what the Bible said about death:

"For the wages of sin is death, but the gift of God is eternal life in Christ Jesus our Lord." (Rom. 6:23)

He'd claimed faith in God early in our marriage but had largely turned his back on church and religion the last several years. I could only hope that though he hadn't "laid up treasures in heaven" (Matt. 6:19) by living a godly life, Tony might have believed and been saved as the apostle Paul described to the Corinthian church:

"If anyone builds on this foundation [faith in Jesus] using gold, silver, costly stones, wood, hay or straw, their work will be shown for what it is, because the day will bring it to light. It will be revealed with fire, and the fire will test the quality of each person's work. If what has been built survives, the builder will receive a reward. If it is burned up, the builder will suffer loss but yet will be saved—even though only as one escaping through the flames." (1 Cor. 3:12–15)

As Luke got older, I'd teach him about God and take him to Sunday school. I wanted him to learn about Jesus giving his life for our sins on the cross and about the urgency of making a personal decision to accept Jesus Christ as his Savior. If I didn't teach him, as God intended, I'd be failing my most important task as a parent.

Tony's brother and sisters had always been kind to me, and I loved them like my own family. So I asked them to go with me to Ocean City, Maryland, to scatter Tony's ashes. Tony loved to fly, so I called around until I found a pilot willing to fly us over the Atlantic Ocean to scatter the ashes. The pilot was retired military, and to my astonishment, he offered to do it for free.

The plane was a four-seater. Tony's brother and one of his sisters accompanied me, sitting in the back while I sat up front. Once we were out over the water, the pilot told us to open the window. The airstream was powerful, grabbing at the bag and trying to rip it out of our hands as we spilled out the ashes. Spreading out behind the plane, they sparkled in the sunlight like a trail of diamonds in the sky.

Tony's sister made a beautiful white cross as a memorial and placed it beside the highway where Tony died. I would go and sit for a while whenever I missed him. Even though we'd had a terrible marriage, we still had some wonderful memories, and I'd loved him dearly, so I chose to remember the good times and forget the bad. In truth, my heart broke more for my son's loss than for my own because I knew how much Luke missed his dad. I grieved for all the moments my son would never have with Tony.

Since I never saw Tony's body, I persisted in feeling he was still alive. A few weeks after the Ocean City trip, Mom and I were at a yard sale when I spotted a man smoking a cigarette. Something about the familiarity of that sight squeezed my heart. Blinking back tears, I didn't realize then why I was so upset. But after that, every time I saw someone holding a cigarette, it made me think of Tony.

On another occasion, I saw a man I thought was Tony in a group of people. I ran up to him, but when he turned around, I realized he was a stranger. This happened many times in many places over the next few years. Maybe the government was lying to me and Tony was really in the witness protection program because he'd testified against some drug kingpin.

Even after Luke stopped expecting Dada to come home, I'd jump any time I heard a car door slam outside, thinking it was him. I wanted him to come home for real, not only in my dreams.

15. Luke's Shenanigans

Even without the example of Dada, Luke showed himself to be a determined little boy. One day, he pointed to the heat vent in the kitchen floor. He said that a small toy had fallen in and he wanted me to get it out. I explained that the toy was gone and he'd have to play with something else.

"Not gone!" he yelled, bursting into tears.

For a good half hour, he sat by the vent crying and yelling, convinced I could find a way to get his toy out. The next day, my employee stopped by the house. When I mentioned the loss, he quickly located a screwdriver and popped the vent cover open. Luke was delighted to get his toy back.

After a heavy snowstorm, I had to shovel the driveway. Bundling Luke up, I took him out to play in the snow. He loved it. That evening, I went upstairs to put clothes away, leaving Luke on the couch watching cartoons. He decided to go back outside to play. The deadbolt was out of his reach, so he carried over his small chair and climbed up to unlock it.

When I came down to get him ready for bed, I found the kitchen door hanging wide-open. Luke was missing. Running outside into the blowing snow, I discovered him standing in the driveway with his tiny toy shovel. He was only wearing a diaper but had managed to put his little boots on.

He looked adorable. But I was worried he'd get sick and end up in the hospital. If something happened to him after losing his father, I didn't know what I'd do. He was the most important person in the world to me.

I was also concerned people would think I was a bad mom for letting my kid out of the house like that. He was so smart. Once he saw you do something, he quickly learned to do it himself. From then on, I had to set the alarm when we were in the house so I'd know if he opened a door. I'd always thought alarms were for protection from someone breaking *in*, not breaking *out*.

A week later, I walked into the kitchen to find Luke sitting by the heat vent with a screwdriver in his hand. He'd pulled the vent cover off and told me his toy was down there. I had to wonder if he was throwing his toys down there intentionally, thinking it was some sort of game. At that moment, I knew the older he got, the more trouble he'd get into.

One day after we cleaned my car, Luke headed indoors. I was just seconds behind him. But in that short time, he'd poured a can of cleanser all over himself and my kitchen floor. I guess he thought it was cleaning day. I decided this was a good time to scrub the kitchen floor. I gave him a rag. Copying me, he got down on his hands and knees, and we scrubbed for the next half hour. I had no idea how he'd gotten the cleanser in the first place since the cupboard was locked with a child safety latch.

Luke and my dad became very close as Dad stayed home on Sunday afternoons to see us. Every time Luke saw his grandfather, he'd beg Dad to pick him up. Then Dad would shake his hair in Luke's face. I don't know why this made Luke laugh uncontrollably, but it did. I couldn't watch them without laughing too.

That Christmas, we went over to my parents' house to open gifts. Every time Luke pulled a piece of wrapping paper off a gift, he'd walk over to the garbage bag we had set out and put it in. He was a neat freak, just like me. Eventually, we moved the garbage bag next to him so he didn't have to walk so far.

Luke turned two that next month. Though determined, he was also obedient. Whenever he did something wrong, I just had to look at him and ask if he wanted a spanking.

"Noooooo," he'd immediately respond and stop what he was doing.

In May, I decided I no longer wanted to run Tony's fieldstone business. I simply turned it over to the manager I'd hired. He was delighted for the opportunity to make the business his own.

In June, Luke started attending Sunday school since at two and a half he was now old enough for the youngest class. His two teachers were fabulous, and Luke loved telling me everything he learned in class. One of the teachers especially, Mr. Najjar, had a significant impact on Luke's life, always praying for him and mentoring him.

Time seemed to be flying by with Luke growing by leaps and bounds. Overall, he was a happy child who smiled a lot, talked a lot, and liked to take care of his toys. What I treasured most was that he always told me that he loved me.

When Luke was three, I bought my first computer from a friend. It came with a bunch of children's games. Luke and I were excited. I wanted Luke to be interested in learning, so I bought him *Bob the Builder* and *Dora the Explorer*, which became his favorites.

Sometime in March, Luke decided to make himself a peanut butter sandwich. After eating it, he painted a picture to surprise me. I must have dozed off in the living room as I didn't see or hear any of this while it was happening. When he finished his painting, he came into the living room to get me.

Following him to the kitchen, I was shocked at what I saw. The cupboards, counter, and vinyl floor were slathered with peanut butter. He'd used the entire jar. I asked why he'd done something so naughty.

"I made you art. It's a pretty picture."

Once again, I had no idea how he could have gotten the peanut butter since it was stored in a cupboard well out of reach. When I asked, he demonstrated how he'd climbed up on the kitchen counter by stepping on the drawer handles of the lower cupboards. I was amazed. He'd make an extraordinary rock climber one day.

I bathed Luke and spent the next two hours scrubbing the kitchen. Even then, everything still felt oily. I told him never to do that again. But he didn't seem to understand there was anything wrong with what he'd done.

For Easter that year, Luke sat at his child's table in the living room coloring a paper Easter egg. He wrote words on it and decorated it with different colors. He told me it was for his Gram and Pap (my parents). He was so excited and kept asking if I thought they'd like it. "Me thinks they'll like it."

He was so intelligent and liked using big words. But it was the little things he said like "me thinks" that made him adorable. Later that afternoon, I was in the kitchen when Luke walked in. His face was colored, and a closer inspection revealed that he'd used markers to color in "eye shadow" on his eyelids. My hoop earrings dangled from his earlobes, and he'd put on my high heels.

"Me beautiful like you, Mommy."

I had to chuckle but felt like crying. I wondered if he was getting the sexes confused and thought he was a girl. I wished he had a father in his life. I could already see difficult times ahead if he didn't have a positive male role model in his life soon.

16. Love Again?

In April 2001, I drove to my parents' house for my sister's bridal shower. After the shower, we were standing in the driveway when I noticed one of the neighbors sitting in his car. Gram stared at him. "That's Mike. You remember him. He's a short good-looking man about six years older than you with blond hair."

"Of course I remember him." I'd known Mike casually for most of my life. With his head held high, Mike strolled over to us. His blue eyes were full of kindness when he said hello.

After I casually mentioned it was my birthday, Mike invited me out for dinner to celebrate. I accepted. Over dinner, we caught up on each other's lives. He knew about Tony's death. I knew he'd married and had kids. He said he'd been separated for some time and was in the process of getting a divorce. He had three kids: fourteen-year-old Alan, eleven-year-old Shawn, and nine-year-old Jessica.

We talked about religion and faith as well. When Mike's marital difficulties first began, they started seeing a Christian counselor. His wife refused to continue after the first visit, but Mike kept going and, through his counselor's influence, had recently placed his faith in Jesus Christ. He and his kids were currently attending a Catholic church.

Mike and I enjoyed being together and agreed to go out again the following weekend. We started seeing each other regularly, although I didn't meet his kids for a few months. We wanted to see how our relationship developed first, and Mike wanted to finalize the divorce before openly dating again.

In June, I was the matron of honor at my sister's wedding. I took Luke as my "date," and we had a wonderful time. Come July, and to my great surprise, Mike told me that he loved me. That August, we let our kids meet. Mike was one of seven siblings, and every summer they rented a beach house in the Outer Banks of North Carolina.

Mike invited Luke and me to join his family for the trip. Each sibling chipped in for part of the rental. Mike made a good salary working for the local water authority and received income from his apartment rentals. He insisted on paying for the room Luke and I shared.

The trip was a bonding time for our two families. Since Luke loved his small sandbox, he'd love the beach even more. Sure enough, he had a great time building castles and digging giant holes with Mike's nephew, who was close to Luke's age. I got along well with Mike's family, and they were all glad to see him happy.

At the end of August, I signed Luke up for preschool. He was excited, but I was concerned how he'd handle being there without me. He was thrilled when he came home, showing me pictures and telling me how he got to be the class leader.

A couple months later, Luke informed me, "Me got a surprise for you."

Oh, boy, what now? He led me up to his bedroom and proudly showed me the artwork on his wall. This time it wasn't peanut butter. I explained to Luke that he wasn't to write on anything other than paper. But I also decided it was time to lock away the markers.

When it was my turn to be a parent helper at school, Luke was so excited he woke me up before the alarm went off. He talked nonstop and introduced me to all his new friends. He got me a drink and crackers at snack time, explaining that he wanted to get there first because if they ran out, you had to choose another snack, and he didn't want his mommy going hungry.

That night, Luke made us dinner to accompany the cartoons we were watching. Laying out slices of bread, he perfectly aligned pieces of popcorn on the bread, then covered them with ketchup. Handing me mine, he ordered, "Eat, Mommy."

The concoction looked disgusting, but he was so excited I ate the whole thing. I'd never seen his smile bigger than it was as I consumed his culinary experiment. That was a precious day I will remember forever.

Luke was still constantly climbing up on the counter to raid the cupboards. He'd sometimes even climb up on the kitchen table and sit there to eat. If I didn't know better, I'd have thought I'd given birth to a monkey.

Meanwhile, I fell head over heels in love with Mike. He was the complete opposite of Tony, and I was thankful for that. He was so kind and loving; he reminded me of an angel. From the moment we reconnected as adults, he became my rock. I could always count on him, and that has never changed.

In October, for Mike's birthday, I snuck into the parking lot of his office building and put two dozen red roses all over his silver Dodge Durango. Several of his coworkers stopped to ask me what was happening since they didn't know it was his birthday. Needless to say, when Mike got off work at 4:00 p.m., there was an audience in the parking lot, including me. I wanted to see his face when he spotted the roses. He liked the surprise even though it embarrassed him.

Despite Mike still waiting for his divorce paperwork to be completed, we were officially dating. We decided to attend the church where the counselor who'd led Mike to Christ attended.

This church was where I learned for the first time that God is not a God of total condemnation and judgment but a God who loves me and wants good things for me. As my heavenly Father, he wants me to know him intimately. Through the Holy Spirit, he lives within me to help me with my daily struggles. This news became life-changing for me, and over the next few years, I grew as a Christ follower.

17. Luke's Troubles

Because I began experiencing trouble with Luke around this time, I needed God's guidance. He wasn't yet four years old when he started exhibiting a terrible temper. His fists hit me like a hailstorm pummels a car. If he didn't get his own way, he'd throw temper tantrums that lasted for hours. Why had he changed so drastically?

Shortly after his fourth birthday in February, Luke received his first bike. Mike's kids all had bikes, and Luke felt left out riding his tricycle or toy jeep. So he was excited for the weather to get nice enough to begin riding. Because there was no place to ride at my house, we kept the bike at my parents' house. It was convenient that Mike lived next door.

Around March, I started to realize something was seriously wrong with Luke. In addition to the tantrums he was overly shy, had major anger issues, and was still hitting me and calling me names. It was impossible to make him sit in a timeout since the only way to stop him was to practically sit on him. Sometimes he would yell at me for no reason and storm out the door.

After dealing with similar behavior from his biological father, I was scared and took Luke to a psychologist. Luke was so belligerent, calling the doctor names and refusing to cooperate, that it was challenging to complete the necessary tests. The psychologist determined that Luke had a very high intelligence level. He suggested many possibilities as to what could be wrong, but he couldn't be sure of any single diagnosis.

Since Luke wouldn't cooperate, I was told not to bring him back because he wasted everyone's time and my money. I didn't care about the money. I just wanted help for my son. If the professionals couldn't help him, what was I supposed to do?

Spring finally came. Luke started riding his bike with training wheels on it, and within a few months, we took the training wheels off. Luke would speed around the neighborhood, yelling, "Mommy, look at me, look at me!"

That June, Mike's divorce was finalized. In July, Mike and I decided we wanted to join the church we were attending. This necessitated taking an eight-week membership orientation class. As part of it, we were required to share our faith story, including how we came to know God.

It was in this class that I recommitted my life to God. Most of my life I'd been living in sin, ever since I'd first made a profession of faith as a Christian at the age of thirteen. Deeply convicted, I found it terribly hard to accept God's forgiveness or forgive myself for all the awful things I'd done—having intimate relationships with older men in my teen years, rebelling against my parents and God, and living out of wedlock with Tony for our first two years.

But I also came to understand how much Jesus loves me. He didn't make me to punish me. He made me with a specific purpose, and he wants me to serve him for the rest of my life. We all have a God-given purpose, and I hoped and prayed I could fulfill mine.

Mike also shared the details of his own salvation experience, and I thanked God for blessing me with such a wonderful Christian man. After hearing about my recommitment, Mike recommitted his life to serving our Lord and Savior.

Since Mike had joint custody, his kids went to Sunday school with us whenever they were with him for the weekend. I prayed daily that they would come to know Christ and surrender their lives to serving God as Mike and I were trying to do. Meanwhile, Luke was at Sunday school every week and could rattle on all about Jesus. I hoped and prayed that my precious son would figure out and fulfill his purpose, much as God once spoke to the prophet Jeremiah:

"Before I formed you in the womb I knew you, before you were born I set you apart; I appointed you as a prophet to the nations." (Jer. 1:5)

One day after church, Mike's daughter Jessica told us she'd asked Jesus into her heart and was now a Christian. The news poured over Mike and me like a warm shower on a cold day. I could not control the tears of joy flowing from my eyes. It is such a relief to know your loved ones will be together with you in heaven for eternity. We will see the angels worshipping Jesus and get to worship him ourselves. There will be pearly gates, golden streets, and a crystal river. There won't be any pain or suffering. I can't wait to go there.

In September, my sister let the family know that she was pregnant. To my dismay, Luke immediately started crying when he found out. We finally figured out he was afraid Jamie wouldn't love him anymore if she had a baby. Jamie explained to him that she'd never run out of love for him no matter how many babies she had.

In any case, there would be plenty of love to go around for Luke. One day in Mike's living room, I spontaneously got down on one knee and grabbed Mike's hand. With tears in my eyes I stuttered, "Mike, you know I love you and I don't want to live my life without you. I know you are afraid to get married again. I promise I will never hurt you, but I can't wait forever for you to decide if you want to marry me. If you love me as I love you, will you marry me?"

Mike's face turned red from embarrassment and tears welled up in his eyes. The silence stretched into endless seconds. Was he going to say no?

After what felt like an eternity, he grabbed my other hand, so he was now holding both of my hands and looked straight into my soul: "I love you with all of my heart, and I know you will never hurt me. Yes, I will marry you." Then he kissed me and pulled me into a tight embrace, whispering in my ear, "I can't imagine my life without you." I was the happiest girl on the planet.

Soon, we began marriage counseling with the pastor of the church we were attending.

We also listed my house for sale, thinking it wouldn't sell right away. When it did, we had a bit of a problem. I didn't want to repeat the mistakes I'd made in the past, and that included not moving in with Mike until we were married. We resolved the problem by moving the wedding to May, right before the new owner closed on the house.

In March, my sister's son Jerry James was born. Luke and I went to the hospital to visit them. Once Luke met JJ, as he was quickly nicknamed, he proved quite happy to have a baby cousin.

For Easter, Luke and Mike's youngest daughter Jessica colored eggs, making some beautiful designs. On Easter morning, we had an egg hunt for Luke and Mike's kids. We assigned each kid a specific egg color and put a certain amount of money along with candy in the eggs. Since Luke was only five, we'd hidden his eggs in easier places, telling the kids that if they came across someone else's eggs, they were to leave them where they found them. Because Mike's kids were much older than Luke, we were surprised when he quickly found their eggs.

Luke became excited, boasting about how he'd spotted their eggs. "Mommy, this is easy. Why didn't you hide them harder?"

My son was growing up, and I certainly had to give him credit for his intelligence. He also loved making up elaborate songs and singing them for me. One day, he came into the room wearing a backward baseball cap and dancing like a rapper as he sang. He must have been copying something he'd seen on TV. He asked me to record him, and he did a phenomenal job.

At the beginning of May, I bought Luke a new bedroom set since he didn't need the toddler bed anymore. We took it to Mike's house so it would be ready after the wedding. In May 2003, Mike and I got married. The wedding was perfect, and Luke looked adorable in his suit. He danced with me at the reception, smiling and excited over getting to stay with my parents while Mike and I were away on our honeymoon.

Mike owned an apartment building as well as a duplex in Sidman, Pennsylvania. We knew that we'd need a bigger place than either of our current homes for our blended family after the wedding. He solved this problem by converting the duplex back into a single-family dwelling. We remodeled the house by updating the bathrooms and kitchen, replacing carpeting, and adding a new master bath and walk-in closet. Mike and I spent a week honeymooning in Jamaica. When we returned, we moved into our new home.

18. BACK TO REALITY

Luke attended a few summer classes to help him prepare for the transition from preschool to kindergarten. He was such a joyous blessing from God but still cried uncontrollably and had anger issues. I was aware he might need medication but couldn't get any psychiatrists or doctors to agree on what was wrong. They speculated on everything from narcissistic personality disorder and ADHD to borderline personality disorder. If I was going to put my son on medicine, I wanted the medical professionals treating him to be sure of his diagnosis.

In July, I told Mike that since he'd covered our beach trip last year, I'd use my time-share this year to book a condo in Hilton Head, South Carolina. We did miss having his entire clan with us, but we enjoyed being together as a blended family. Luke loved playing in the sand with his stepsiblings.

That fall, Luke started kindergarten. He was excited to ride the big yellow school bus. For preschool, there'd only been a small bus. At the end of his first day, he gave me a huge hug and told me he'd missed me. He said he liked riding the big bus because it didn't have seat belts. His favorite activity that day was coloring. It was bittersweet to see my little boy growing up and becoming so independent.

For Christmas, Luke received a robot and a remote-controlled jeep. Knowing how we can lose loved ones without notice, I videotaped his holiday highlights as I'd done since he was born. I couldn't contain my laughter when he looked sternly into the camera. "I'm talking to the people who might watch this, Mommy, not you."

That February, our pastor baptized Mike and me by immersion in a joint baptism service. Joyfully, we professed our personal belief in Jesus Christ as our Lord and Savior in front of the church. Being immersed under the water symbolizes the death of our old self, while emerging from the water symbolizes our new life in Christ cleansed from our sins (Rom. 6:3–5; Col. 2:12–13). It was so wonderful to share this experience with Mike, my amazing new husband, my best friend.

In April, Luke was old enough to start memorizing Bible verses. He was very good at it and so proud of himself every time he got one right. I began reading him daily devotions from *Our Daily Bread*, which I received in the mail every month. Each day's reading contained a short story, Bible passage, and a prayer. He enjoyed them, especially the stories. Every night I'd pray with Luke.

For our first anniversary, Mike and I traveled to the Dominican Republic, where I'd booked an all-inclusive time-share at a beach resort. For the first two days, everything was beautiful. On the third day, I woke up with severe pain in my stomach. Mike called the resort nurse. In broken English mixed with Spanish, she told me I needed to go to the hospital. She called a taxi, shoving Mike and me into it. "Go! Now!"

There they ran a few tests, then told me I probably had appendicitis and would need immediate surgery as my appendix could rupture at any time. I saw Mike blinking back tears as he pretended to look out the window. Neither Mike nor I thought it was safe to get surgery in a foreign country with medical personnel who didn't speak our language. Finally, another doctor who spoke better English came in and did a more thorough exam. He determined it wasn't appendicitis, just a stomach virus from something I ate or drank. Relieved but concerned, I refused to eat or drink much for the rest of our stay. I was thrilled to get back on US soil.

My little boy continued to grow. That summer, I took Luke as well as Mike's kids regularly to the pool. By the end of summer, Luke was swimming like a fish. We again took the kids to a beach time-share for a family vacation. Luke had started first grade and was nervous and upset because he didn't know most of his classmates. In November, I took him on a mother-son trip to Disney World. He kept me awake all night, telling me what he wanted to do the next day at the park. He had the time of his life.

Mike met us at the airport a few days later with flowers for me and a big hug for Luke. On the ride home, I listened to Luke telling Mike everything we'd done. I was so happy to see how he was getting along with his stepdad. I couldn't have asked for a better person to be a role model for my son. Mike was a saint and loved Luke as much as he loved his own kids, even if Luke's behavior sometimes made it hard to love him.

In August, Luke started second grade. He came home excited to have art, music, and gym but was not happy about reading. The only time Luke read was when someone forced him. He couldn't wait for the second day of school. He even called me to his room to say his prayers early. "If I go to bed, then school will come quicker."

I'd been praying with him for over a year now, and he'd really learned a lot. It was amazing to hear him pray, "God, please take care of me, Mommy, and my family. Bless my friends and teachers, and thank you for them."

By the third week of school, Luke asked, "Mom, will you please pack my lunch? I don't like the cafeteria food. Make me a peanut butter and jelly sandwich every day." I included fruit roll-ups and a juice box and put money in his lunch account in case he wanted milk.

I met with Luke's teacher for an in-service appointment to discuss Luke's progress. He informed me, "Luke is doing well, especially in math. If all my students were like him, I'd have no problems." I was so proud of Luke. I couldn't wait to tell him. It would definitely make him smile.

I continued to be amazed at Luke's drawing skills as well. He was also creative at making up songs. Maybe he'd become a writer or graphic designer one day. For Thanksgiving, his class made a paper turkey they colored for their parents. Luke made one for Mike and me and wrote his own Thanksgiving message on it: "I am thankful for my mom and dad who take care of me. I am thankful for my food because it helps me live. I am thankful for my grandma and Pap and Aunt Jamie. I am thankful that my grandma is feeling better. Thanksgiving makes me feel great."

I taped that paper in Luke's milestones scrapbook so I could treasure it forever. Then, the following week, I explained the gospel in detail to Luke. I told him that the only way to be saved is through grace. There isn't any way to earn our salvation by being good.

"For it is by grace you have been saved, through faith—and this is not from yourselves, it is the gift of God—not by works, so that no one can boast." (Eph. 2:8–9)

When Luke made the personal decision that he wanted to become a Christian, tears of sheer joy streamed down my cheeks. Since he was only seven years old, I helped him formulate the words. Together, we prayed: "Dear Jesus, I believe in you. I believe you are the Son of God, that you died for my sins, and that you were buried and rose again as written in the Bible. Please come into my heart so I can have eternal life. Fill me with the Holy Spirit and help me to live the way you want me to live. Forgive me for my past sins. Guide me in my future so that I can live my life for you. Amen."

19. Serving God Together

With Luke excelling in school, I decided to get my real estate license. I studied hard and scored high on the test. I was proud of myself and excited to get started. It was winter, a difficult time for sales in Pennsylvania, but I sold my first house in January just before Luke's eighth birthday. It wasn't a huge commission, but I was happy to be making progress.

By April, I'd sold five houses. One of the listings was a newly built house. When my dad saw the sign in the yard with my picture on it, he told me he was very proud of me. My heart melted like butter on a hot stove. Luke was excited for me too, but also upset because real estate meant working a lot in the evenings and on weekends. So when Luke asked me to spend more time with him, I started scheduling one day off per week to accomplish this.

One day, I was again videotaping Luke when he looked me in the eye. "Can I have a moment of peace? I'm doing my hair."

I laughed and laughed. Luke styled his hair every day, even when school let out for the summer. In July, we took a blended family vacation to an all-inclusive Bahamas resort. It was the first time Mike's kids had been on an airplane. Having flown before, Luke was excited for them and loved that he was the "expert" in this experience. The kids had never been at an all-inclusive resort, so they were astounded at all the food available and that they could go snorkeling or out on a kayak any time they wanted. Now I had a family who loved to travel as much as I did.

That fall, my real estate sales slowed to one in October and one in December. But this allowed me to spend more time with Luke, so I considered it a blessing.

In May, Mike and I attended a class at church that helped match our talents and spiritual gifts to various areas of serving God. I was good at administration, faith, giving, and helping. I felt God calling me to volunteer with a Christian nonprofit organization that helps children in developing countries get an education. So I began doing a lot of administrative work for them.

Mike and I also decided to sponsor a little girl named Mya from a low-income family in Jamaica. From our sponsorship, she received her school uniform and supplies, an educational scholarship, and one hot meal a day. For some of these children, this was the only meal they received since Jamaica is a very poor country.

By now, it had become apparent that I wasn't good at setting boundaries for work. I always made myself available to my clients, and whether midnight or early morning, I'd jump out of bed to answer my phone. Mike suggested I give up real estate and find something else to do or simply quit and not look for another job. Unlike my years with Tony when I was the main breadwinner, Mike was financially stable, so it wasn't necessary that I work.

That summer, after finishing fourth grade, Luke asked to get a pet. I had noticed a nearby farm had kittens to give away, so Mike and I took Luke to pick out a cat. Kayley was supposed to be an outside cat, but she kept going onto the main road. Luke was worried she'd get hit by a car, so she became an indoor cat. Luke carried her everywhere. He was so gentle and loving with her. He loved Kayley more than life itself, which was all that mattered to me as I loved my son more than life itself and would do anything for him.

Luke got along well with Mike's kids but especially his stepsister Jessica. They hung out for hours, riding bikes, playing video games, swimming, watching movies, or playing with Kayley. They loved each other like true blood siblings, and Jessica always looked out for Luke since she was six years older. By now, Luke was calling Mike "Dad" and seemed to genuinely enjoy spending time with his family. He liked making people happy and was always telling jokes to make everyone laugh.

Around the time Luke turned eleven, I bought a lot of Rock Band games for Luke's Xbox so Luke and I could play together. Luke liked to play guitar and could sing and play the drums. I sang too if what I did could be called singing. I also taught myself to play the drums a little, and Luke and I spent many hours laughing at the terrible music we created. I will always cherish those memories.

That following spring, I began substituting as needed at the elementary school cafeteria. I enjoyed the job and made a lot of friends. Even better, I got to see Luke and his friends, who thought it was cool having Luke's mom working in the cafeteria.

That May, I felt God's call to participate in a missions trip to the site in Jamaica where Mike and I were sponsoring a child. At eleven years old, Luke was underage for such a trip. Since I was a long-term volunteer with the organization and would personally supervise him, I was allowed to take Luke with me. He was excited to go and that we'd finally be able to meet our sponsor child, Mya.

I explained to Luke that to go, we'd need to raise two thousand dollars by October. We sent out donor request letters to friends and family as well as our church, asking for their support on our journey. Luke helped me write the letters. We each signed them. I encouraged Luke to open the mail each day to check for any responses. Donations began rolling in. It was wonderful to share this faith experience with Luke. I explained that if God calls you to do something, he will provide the means just as Jesus promised:

"So I say to you: ask and it will be given to you; seek and you will find; knock and the door will be opened to you." (Luke 11:9)

One day, we were heading out to do some shopping. I pulled the mail from the mailbox and handed it to Luke since I was driving. He anxiously opened one of our response letters and announced that we'd received another check for our trip.

"How much is it for?"

Yanking on my arm, he answered, "Five hundred dollars."

I was astonished. "Are you sure there are two zeros and that it isn't fifty dollars?"

"No, it's for five hundred dollars."

I pulled the car over to take a look for myself. Sure enough, it was a check for five hundred dollars from a couple who attended the same church class as Mike and me. With tears of joy filling my eyes, I pulled back onto the road. Luke grabbed my arm again, yelling, "Do we have enough money? Are we able to go on the trip?"

"Yes, Luke. God has provided the money we need. We are going to Jamaica! We have met our goal of two thousand dollars." It was a valuable spiritual lesson for Luke. If I hadn't let him help with the letters and opening the mail, he wouldn't have gotten to experience God's blessings and generosity firsthand.

That fall, Luke complained about starting the sixth grade. In fact, he no longer wanted to attend school at all. However, when October came, his mood improved significantly since none of his eleven-year-old friends had ever been on a missions trip, much less to Jamaica. Though it meant missing class, Luke's school permitted me to take him as an educational trip, and I felt it was important for Luke to witness for himself and serve those less privileged, as God calls us to do:

"Truly I tell you, whatever you did for one of the least of these brothers and sisters of mine, you did for me." (Matt. 25:40)

When our team arrived in Jamaica, Luke changed into his white scrubs. We drove to the Jamaican School for the Deaf, where our project included painting the facility. I also taught a Bible class to the children. Luke hid behind me when we were around the other volunteers but not when we were around the children we were there to help. He hugged them and laughed with them and wasn't the least bit shy. I hadn't seen him this relaxed in a long time and felt blessed to be a part of it all.

The next day we met our sponsor child. Mya's eyes sparkled like distant lakes in the sunshine when we presented her with the coloring books, crayons, paper, and other educational supplies we'd brought. She immediately shared everything we'd given her with other children in the classroom. Later that night, Luke grabbed my hands and asked me, "Mom, would it be all right if I sell my Xbox and give the money to these kids?"

I knew how much Luke treasured his Xbox, so this was a huge step for him. Our relationship before this trip had been a little strained. We were now bonding again in ways I could never have imagined, and I could see God making real progress in Luke's heart. I loved every moment I got to spend with my son and our sponsor child Mya.

We also visited an orphanage, where we held Vacation Bible School for the older children. One of the volunteers taught Luke how to use his camera. Smiling from ear to ear, Luke took pictures of all of the children. I could tell how proud he was to be trusted with such an expensive piece of equipment. His love for the children was written all over his face. He'd get down on his knees to help them color or complete one of the many crafts we'd brought for the kids.

In the afternoon, we visited the nursery for babies and younger children. With so few employees and so many children, the toddlers and babies received little human contact and wanted to be held. We'd pick one kid up, and two more would hang on our legs, wanting to be picked up too.

Holding more than one kid was hard, so Luke sat down on the floor. At least two kids sat on his lap, and two more hung on his back. Sweat poured from his forehead onto his scrubs, but nothing could hide his smile. It was not something either of us would soon forget. After story time, we took turns holding the babies that were in their cribs. When it was time to leave, I had to pull Luke out of the orphanage. It was heartbreaking that these children had no parents. Luke's tears soaked my shirt as I held him on the way back to the hotel.

At home, Luke shared stories with Mike. He begged Mike to sell his Xbox and send the money to the orphanage children, but Mike said no and instead sent money. I was so amazed at the difference this trip had made in Luke. He was more outgoing instead of being shy. He hugged Mike and me every day and he constantly told us he loved us.

The remainder of the school year went well, with Luke still outstandingly carefree. He loved playing with his cat, whom he'd greatly missed while we were away. He was always laughing and making jokes. I felt so blessed that he was happy.

20. Teen Slump

Seventh grade started well, but then Luke became increasingly lazy about keeping his room clean. He peed in two-liter soda bottles rather than walking to the bathroom right outside his bedroom door. I'd find plates and bowls in his room with dried and moldy food, and the air smelled like sweat. I finally told Luke he couldn't have food or drinks in his room, but he took them up when I wasn't watching.

That October, Mike and I decided to go on the same missions trip to Jamaica Luke and I had taken the year before. I asked Luke if he wanted to go. His heart had been so touched the last time he went, and I'd definitely seen God working in him, so I was hoping for more positive changes. But Luke said no, and I didn't want to force him to go.

We asked my mom if Luke could stay with her for the week we'd be away. She was happy to spend time with him. Mike and I saw God's love and the Holy Spirit's power working in so many people during the trip. The smiles on the children's faces when we gave them something as simple as a glass of water was the most impactful sign of that power.

When we arrived home, Luke was thrilled to see me. He grabbed my arm and pulled me out to my dad's garage. He handed me a hook with a towel covering something underneath it, which he said was a gift for me. Tears filled my eyes as I removed the towel. I was astonished at seeing a gorgeous wooden birdhouse. Dad helped Luke make it for me. I brushed at the moisture now forming heavily on my lashes. I knew I would treasure this thoughtful gift from my son and my dad.

In November, though Luke was only twelve years old, he began his first girlfriend relationship. She was two grades ahead of him. Mike and I had no idea what was going on, and he was once again having a lot of problems at school. He was getting poor grades on tests, and his teachers told me he wasn't doing his homework. He was also giving me a hard time at home, swearing at me and refusing to obey. I didn't know what to do.

One night, we had a terrible fight, and he stormed out of the house. The temperature was below zero, so I was worried sick. He had his cell phone with him, but he was so angry that he texted he was turning off his phone and would see me in the morning when he came home.

I called the police. The next day when Luke finally came home, an officer arrived at our house. Introducing himself, he handed Luke his business card. Luke took the card, tore it up, and threw it back at the officer. Angry, the officer made Luke hand over his cell phone. Calling the last number dialed, he discovered that Luke had been with his girlfriend, Johanna, all night at her dad's house.

That was how we found out about the relationship. I'd made my mistakes with Tony, and I was deeply grateful God had forgiven me. But I couldn't imagine what kind of dad would let his teenage daughter have a boy sleep over, especially a twelve-year-old. Luke was outraged at the police officer for exposing his relationship. In the end, the ninth grader broke up with him.

Luke missed so many days of seventh grade he almost reached the maximum allowed without failing the grade. We had major arguments every morning trying to get him on the bus. I tried bribing him, grounding him, taking away his Xbox and phone. Nothing seemed to work. I even called the police at one point. They informed me that I could receive a fine if the school didn't have an excuse for Luke's absences.

What I didn't realize was that Luke had become suicidal over his breakup with the ninth grader. He hid behind his long hair so I couldn't see his expressions. At length, I heard him making sniffling noises, and I assumed he was crying. Even when I bought him his favorite food or gave him a gift, he didn't seem to notice anything. He wore a blank expression and he was extremely depressed. Every time I tried to talk to him, he yelled at me, hit me, or broke things.

Then in January, one of his friends called to tell me Luke had threatened to kill himself. I immediately took Luke to the hospital. I tried to talk to the doctor through my constricted throat, but nothing could be heard. Finally, the doctor admitted Luke into the psychiatric ward. He was furious, begging me to take him home. I told him I couldn't, but if he listened to the doctors and learned how to process his feelings and cope with stress, they'd release him.

He was released later that week and seemed better for a while. The hospital scheduled follow-up counseling sessions, but after a few sessions, Luke wouldn't go back. Trying to make him go only resulted in huge arguments that put a serious strain on our relationship, so I quit fighting with him about it.

Around this time, Luke started having trouble seeing the blackboard in class. His teacher wanted to move him to the front of the class, but he refused. I had his eyes checked and found out that he had astigmatism, which necessitated getting reading glasses. But within days of getting them, Luke insisted he was getting headaches from the glasses. I found out later that he was embarrassed by how they made him look, so he simply refused to wear them.

I continued working as a substitute in the school cafeteria. In early 2011, I was hired full-time for the cafeteria at Luke's middle school. In elementary school, he'd thought it was cool having his mom work in the cafeteria. It wasn't cool anymore in middle school, and Luke instructed me not to talk to him or his friends. I think he was worried I'd embarrass him.

But Luke still liked spending time with me in the evenings and on weekends. We played a lot of Chinese checkers and other games. We were both competitive, and he usually beat me at the games we played. I think he was simply more intelligent than me.

When Luke asked to hang out at a friend's house or go to the mall, I would tell him he could go if he cleaned his room. I started doing random checks and grounding him if his room wasn't clean. But it did no good because he simply didn't care. His room was so disgusting it got to the point he was grounded indefinitely. I just couldn't get through to him. Mike and I suspected that he still had some mental issues, but he refused to seek help. He sat on the couch for hours and always had a dazed look.

It was around this time that Luke started using marijuana, though I didn't learn about it until a few years later. Sadly, he was following in his father's footsteps, and I'd seen what drugs had done to Tony. I wanted better for my only child.

Mike, Luke, and I were still going to church every week as we had since before Mike and I were married. We loved our church so much that we hosted a small group in our home every Wednesday evening. Luke was no longer attending Sunday school and didn't want to attend the church youth group that met Sunday evenings. But he attended the main worship service with us on Sunday mornings. Mike's kids were all adults now and had moved into their own places, so they no longer attended church with us.

In November, my ninety-three-year-old grandmother passed away in her sleep. I was heartbroken as we'd been incredibly close. At her funeral service, I read the following beautiful poem about dying by the clergyman, poet, and author Henry van Dyke, which I'd come across April 24, 2008, in an *Our Daily Bread* devotional titled "A Sailing Ship":

I am standing upon the seashore. A ship at my side spreads her white sails to the morning breeze and starts for the blue ocean. She is an object of beauty and strength. I stand and watch her until at length she hangs like a speck of white cloud, just where the sea and sky come to mingle with each other.... And just at the moment when someone at my side says: "There, she is gone!" there are other eyes watching her coming, and other voices ready to take up the glad shout: "Here she comes!" And that is dying.

I am deeply thankful Gram knew Jesus Christ as her Lord and Savior and that I will see her again one day in heaven. I just hope that I will be laying up as many rewards and crowns as she did in her life for when I finally get to meet Jesus face-to-face. What a joyous day that will be.

21. ARRESTED!

By ninth grade, school wasn't going any better for Luke. Despite his high intelligence, Luke was still skipping many days and refusing to do his homework. He was terribly depressed, and I didn't know if I could keep fighting these battles for another four years, and get him to graduation. The arguing and fighting over homework and attendance put a strain on our relationship that I wasn't sure we had any kinship left.

Many times, he would actually do his homework but not bother to turn it in. Who in their right mind wastes all that time doing the work but refuses to turn it in? It seemed like he was trying to punish me for making him go to school by not turning in the homework because he knew how much that would upset me.

I liked seeing Luke at school every day when he came through the lunch line. But after having surgery for an ongoing health issue, I quit my cafeteria job. With summer approaching, Mike and I decided I should wait before looking for another job since we couldn't trust Luke to be home alone all day.

That summer, Luke started sneaking out of the house. At fifteen years old, he was the same age I'd been when I started sneaking out of my parents' house. He found a way to get around our security system so he could slip out to party with friends and get high. When I found out, I tried grounding him. Rage filled Luke's body as he threw a brand-new cell phone across the room at me. It barely missed my head and smashed against a wall. Sweat poured down his red face and I knew he wanted to hurt me. It felt like not even God could extinguish my pain.

The next day Luke punched our microwave and glass shattered all over the floor. When Luke broke the microwave, Mike and I weren't home. Luke called, and through his slurred words, he said it was broken. He was high or drunk or both. Concerned, Mike and I hurried home. Entering the kitchen, I saw that Luke had managed to clean up most of the glass from the broken microwave. But there was no sign of Luke, so I went into his bedroom to see if he was there.

Meanwhile, Mike headed into the living room. He immediately yelled for me. Rushing in, I saw Luke lying face down on the floor. My mind went immediately to seeing Tony lying on the floor in his diabetic seizures and all the times I'd thought he was going to die. Now the cycle was repeating itself with my son. Luke was becoming Tony.

I can't go through this again. I barely made it through the first time.

I heard a noise like trees blowing in an approaching tornado. Maybe it was the pounding of my heart. I don't know. But if you've ever seen a tree in the path of a tornado, my mind was spinning in the same way. My heart was racing so hard I couldn't breathe. I felt like a feather in the middle of the tornado.

Luke's head was thrust between our loveseat and a bookcase. I couldn't see his face. My first assumption was that he'd passed out or was looking for his cat, who always hid behind the loveseat. I touched him lightly on his back, not wanting him to wake up with a jerk and hit his head since there was no room for him to move. Mike kept saying his name without getting any response. Tornado-forced winds continued to rush through my mind, and we were about to call an ambulance when he started moving. I breathed a sigh of relief.

Luke got up slowly, staggering and swaying all over the place. I tried to get him to sit down and asked him what happened. He shrugged me off angrily and kept saying he was fine. We never learned exactly what was wrong, but he settled down and seemed okay as time passed.

I was disheartened. I'd been doing my best to raise Luke with godly principles so he wouldn't turn out like Tony or me. But it sure didn't seem like I was doing a good job. As the time approached for Luke to go back to school, I began looking for work again. Since I'd had a real estate license in the past and knew a lot about that industry, I was excited to see a job posting for a secretary at a local real estate company. I called for an interview, and they squeezed me in the next morning.

I arrived at the office in my nicest blue suit. They were already finalizing interviews and told me they'd be making their decision that same day. A couple hours later, I received a call asking when I could start. I found out later they had someone else in mind for the position but hired me because of my real estate experience. God's timing is impeccable.

I was blessed again when school started. Luke was now in tenth grade and decided to take an auto body and collision repair class at the vocational school near us. This meant spending half the school day at the local high school and half in the auto body class. He excelled at the vocational school and discovered that he loved working on cars. Finally, something at school Luke enjoyed.

The only thing that bothered Luke was when the teacher told him how to do something, and he wanted to do it his way instead. Luke hated being told how to do anything. He liked being given instructions and left alone to complete the work. Even when he was cleaning at home, if I tried to tell him how to do something, he'd storm out of the room, yelling at me to just do it myself.

I tried again to get him to go to counseling for his anger. I couldn't handle it anymore. Raising his fists at me he screamed, "If you make me go to counseling, I will leave home and you will never see me again." It got to the point that Mike was worried Luke would hurt me. As it was, he'd punch the wall next to me to avoid hitting me, which resulted in Mike having to patch several holes.

Every day I walked on eggshells around Luke. I watched my tone and tried to figure out how to best approach him when something needed to be said. He may have loved his cat more than he loved me, but I knew I was the most important person in the world to him. After every fight, he'd apologize. "Mom, I'm sorry. I love you. I don't know why I do the things I do, but I can't control myself."

For a while, I made him start counseling again. I was relieved that he didn't run away as he'd threatened. But the counselor finally told me she wasn't getting anywhere with him and that with the friction it was causing between Luke and me to get him there, I shouldn't bring him back. She believed it was more important for Luke and me to get along than for him to go to counseling.

That Christmas, we bought Luke a 2005 blue Subaru Legacy. He'd contributed a significant portion of the cost from savings he'd earned doing odd jobs. Though he was only fifteen, we wanted him to learn to drive in the same car he'd be driving after getting his license. Since his dad had died in a car accident, I was paranoid about losing Luke that way too.

For Luke's sixteenth birthday, he was looking forward to driving his new car. He passed his driving permit test on the first try. Then I began taking Luke on practice drives. He claimed to have already driven a car several times, which of course, he shouldn't have, but it was clear he knew what he was doing. Unfortunately, he got confused at stop signs about who had the right-of-way or when he could make a right turn on red. Also, he never followed the speed limit but drove too slow or way too fast. There was no happy medium with Luke.

That May, Mike and I went away for a long weekend to celebrate our anniversary. We'd just checked into a condo when my cell phone rang. I almost fell over when the caller ID said it was the police. I immediately answered. The male voice informed me that my son was in custody for running someone over with a car.

While trying to keep my dinner down, I nervously asked to talk to my son. Luke told me he borrowed his cousin's red Chevy to meet a teenager who owed him money for an ounce of marijuana. Although I couldn't believe what I was hearing, I immediately told Luke to stop talking and tell the officer he wanted an attorney.

I was in total disbelief. I had no idea my son was using, much less selling, marijuana. Once again, I was having flashbacks of the nightmare I had lived with Tony. Luke was becoming his father, and I didn't know how to break the vicious cycle.

The officer's main concern was that a teenager was in the hospital, so I asked Luke to finish his story. Scared, Luke's barely audible voice said the teenager tried to attack him, so he drove away while the teenager was hanging onto the car door. However, he wouldn't let go, so Luke started driving faster. Eventually, he fell. Luke insisted he hadn't run him over.

Terrified for my son, I didn't want him to spend a night in jail. Calling my mom, I asked if she'd pick Luke up at the police station. After the initial shock of learning that her grandson had been arrested, she nervously agreed to pick him up. Since it was already late, Mike and I stayed at the condo that night. To escape my pain, I tried to go to sleep. We returned home first thing in the morning.

When we got home, I spoke to the officer again. The investigation had clarified that Luke didn't run the other kid over, but the kid did have a concussion and was threatening to press charges. Since Luke was a minor, we'd be responsible for any costs, including the fines and costs involved for Luke's six months of probation. We'd have to wait and see if any charges were pressed against Luke.

I made it clear to Luke there were consequences for his actions, starting with being grounded from TV, computer, Xbox, and cell phone unless he was with me. When his anger subsided, Luke opened up to me about his feelings. Through tears he said, "I felt threatened but wasn't trying to hurt anyone." I assured him of my love and firmly stated that he'd have to pay me back for any fines resulting from his recklessness.

22. Wrecks and More Wrecks

Luke finished tenth grade despite missing thirty-three days. Mike and I had planned a vacation that June to a time-share in the Bahamas. With everything going on, we weren't comfortable trusting Luke to stay out of trouble if we left him at home, so I told him he was coming with us.

Luke complained about the long car ride to the airport. I made it clear this was the consequence of his actions and choices, and I prayed he wouldn't ruin the trip for Mike and me. I commiserated with Luke because of the sound of the bratty kid kicking the back of Luke's seat on the plane.

Once we reached our time-share, Luke asked for the Wi-Fi password so he could get on his phone. Since he wasn't complaining, I felt blessed. We rented a boat, thinking that would be fun for Luke. The water was gorgeous, and I could see Luke daydreaming as he stared out over the clear turquoise ocean. But when we stopped at an island for lunch, Luke refused to get off the boat.

Mike finally told him to just stay on the boat. I started crying, not wanting to leave Luke alone in the heat. After much arguing, I convinced Luke to go with us to eat, but he refused to talk to us at lunch and wouldn't eat. I again started crying.

Then Mike noticed Luke staring out at the beautiful ocean with a slight grin on his face. Touching my leg, Mike unobtrusively gestured toward Luke. By the time we left the restaurant, Luke was in a much better mood. Luke beamed as Mike taught him how to operate the boat.

That afternoon, Luke fished for a few hours. Mike snorkeled, finding a huge starfish. Luke's eyes locked on like magnets to the starfish's many feet. He asked me to take a few pictures before putting it back into the ocean. The week went quickly for Mike and me, but I'm sure it was long for Luke. He was happy when it was time to go home.

Whenever Luke got stressed, he'd ask if we could go out for a ride in his car. But, since he only had his driving permit, he wasn't allowed to drive unless I accompanied him. He said driving relaxed him, but it didn't feel that way to me since he always yelled at the other drivers. He was conspicuously paranoid and would insist the other drivers were deliberately tailgating him or staring at him.

One day while driving, Luke got upset and started speeding extremely fast. I was sure he was going to kill us. He told me he didn't want to live anymore and why didn't I just let him kill himself. He said it was all my fault he was still alive. If I'd just mind my own business, he wouldn't have to feel all this pain.

I was terrified and couldn't figure out why Luke was acting this way. Maybe he'd taken some drugs other than marijuana or some laced marijuana. I finally got him to pull into a Dairy Queen parking lot by telling him I had to use the bathroom or I'd wet myself.

Running into the bathroom, I called Mike. He said not to get back into the car with Luke. Heading back to the car, I told Luke, "You can't drive right now. You need to calm down before I let you behind the wheel."

"That's not fair. It's my car. I should be allowed to do what I want with it and drive it whenever I feel like it!" He finally climbed out of the car and stormed off down the road.

I was so thankful for Mike. He is a saint and didn't deserve all the baggage I'd brought into our marriage. When I called Mike again, he counseled me to give Luke time to cool down, then try to find him and bring him home. I waited five minutes, then drove down the road where he'd sprinted off, but I couldn't find him.

After driving around for twenty minutes, I headed home. Shockingly, Luke was already there when I arrived. He wouldn't tell me how he got home, but I assumed he'd hitchhiked as I'd done as a teenager. He didn't speak much to me for the next few weeks, and I stayed out of his way. Then one day, he walked into the room and started talking as though nothing had ever happened. He eventually apologized, explaining that he was under a lot of stress.

"A kid your age shouldn't have that much stress in his life. You know I'm always here for you if you want to talk. I promise I'll never judge you."

He gave me a big hug. "I know, Mom. I love you."

"I love you too," I said, hugging him back.

He broke into a big smile. Then we made dinner together. Luke liked to cook. He made grilled cheese sandwiches and fried potatoes. He also enjoyed making virgin strawberry daiquiris, French toast, and no-bake cookies. But his favorite thing to make was his spicy homemade salsa.

Things went better for a while. Luke had signed up for a drivers' ed class through the school. This required going to the high school for six days straight to complete his supervised driving instruction. He wasn't happy about doing it, especially during summer break. But since completion would give us a discount on our auto insurance, I told him he had to do it or I wouldn't let him get his driver's license.

He completed the course and brought his certificate home so I could give it to our insurance company. We then scheduled his driving test, but he failed it. He made me reschedule it at the earliest permitted time, which was one week later. Once again, he failed.

Angry, he announced that he didn't need his license and even quit practicing. I let it go for a while, then purchased a computerized driving practice program. I had him complete a bunch of practice tests on the computer. Then we started driving again.

He enjoyed driving but wasn't very good at it. I came to believe that whatever was wrong with him mentally was affecting his driving. He couldn't concentrate and constantly went too fast or too slow. Maybe it was better he didn't have a license yet because I wasn't sure I'd ever feel comfortable about him driving on his own. Still, I figured he'd get better with practice, so I didn't give up.

One week at church, Luke slouched in the pew tapping his feet. I don't think I knew anyone who fidgeted more. If Luke wasn't picking at his scabbed arms, he was biting his fingernails, yawning as if it bored him to do so. A staff member said hello to Luke by extending his hand. Luke begrudgingly shook the man's hand, trying to hide his bloody fingernails. Then, the man said something that upset Luke. Getting up, he stormed out of the crowded church. Mike told me to let him go so he could calm down. He was home when we got there but refused to talk about it. The next week, he refused to go to church. Mike and I tried for several weeks to get Luke to return, but he said if we made him go, he'd make a scene and leave. Mike and I prayed for Luke daily, but we didn't know how to help him.

In August, Luke started eleventh grade. He had a few other classes along with auto body for half of his school day. I was hoping he wouldn't give me such a hard time with attendance as in past years.

In October, after several months of practicing, Luke decided to take his driver's test one last time. He told me that he'd never take the test or drive again if he didn't pass this time. I prayed that he would pass, and he did. As soon as we got home, he asked to take the car, so I gave him the car keys since he'd paid most of the car's cost himself. The only condition was that he wasn't to take the car without asking Mike or me first.

Luke wanted to drive to school. One cold, snowy day, he missed the bus, so I let him take the car. When he got to school, there weren't any parking spaces left. He called to tell me he'd have to park on one of the streets surrounding the school. Looking at my watch, I told him to park it anywhere since he couldn't afford another tardy, and I'd come and move it. He made it to class just in time. Meanwhile, I had to find the car, dig it out of the snow pile where he'd parked it, and then get to my job. What a mother will do because she loves her son.

One day in December, the weather turned horrible. The roads were so icy I was surprised the schools didn't close early. I was at work when I received a text from Luke that is every mother's nightmare. It simply said, "I wrecked." Terrified, I called Luke. He answered immediately.

"Are you okay? Is anyone else hurt?"

"I'm fine. No one else is hurt. No one's even around."

"How bad is the car?"

"Not bad. I can drive it home."

"Fine, just drive carefully." I left work immediately and rushed home. The car looked fine to me, and Luke didn't have a mark on him. I asked why he was driving when the roads were so bad and he hadn't asked permission. He didn't answer me since he knew he'd done wrong.

It appeared he slid off the road and overcorrected, hitting a guardrail. When Mike got home from work, he checked the car and told us the frame was bent, which meant the car was totaled. Luke and I were both distraught.

The insurance company confirmed that the car was indeed totaled and sent us a check. I deducted the money Mike and I had invested in the car as well as the insurance cost, then put aside the balance toward another car for Luke. In the meantime, he was grounded.

We eventually found a 2008 white Subaru Impreza. Luke was furious that we hadn't allowed him to pick out his car since he was spending his own money. We told him he could pick out the car he wanted once he got a job and started paying his insurance and repair bills. He was so upset he barely drove this car.

One day, Luke asked if he could take the car and meet some friends at a pool hall. We agreed. I gave him money to play for a few hours and get a snack since he still didn't have a job. He wasn't even looking, and with his antisocial issues, the chances of getting a job were slim.

A few hours later, he called to tell me he'd backed into a parked truck. I was pretty upset until I remembered that I'd done the exact same thing when I was his age. Mike and I talked to the owner and paid for the damages instead of turning it in to the insurance company. It ended up costing us over two thousand dollars.

23. ARRESTED AGAIN

By now Luke was consuming a lot of alcohol and using marijuana heavily. I suspected he was still selling it as well, though he insisted he wasn't. Nor could we trust his word that he wasn't using anything more potent than marijuana. He could have been high when he backed into the parked truck. Mike commented that his eyes appeared glassy when we picked him up. Backing into a parked vehicle in a fairly empty lot took some doing when the parking lot had a width of three car lengths.

One day during school hours, I received a call from the Drug Enforcement Administration (DEA). It was a courtesy call telling me they'd arrested Luke. I fell into an abyss. My heart broke, and I wanted to die. Luke had taken money for a marijuana sale from an undercover police officer, then never returned with the promised marijuana. His friend said the school was locked down and several police officers barged into a full classroom. Locating Luke, his face turned beet red from embarrassment as everyone gasped. The officers demanded he empty his pockets and dump the contents of his backpack. They proceeded to do a pat down, which enraged Luke. In handcuffs, they escorted him out of the school. Knowing how extremely shy Luke was, I was terribly nauseated for him. It took me several hours to track down where they'd taken him, a juvenile detention facility near our house.

I spent the night crying uncontrollably. Mike didn't know how to comfort me. He knew I wanted to help, but Luke was out of control and getting worse. We didn't want to tell him he couldn't live with us, but neither did we know how much longer we could handle him when he refused to obey our rules. We both had this awful feeling that something terrible was going to happen. We worried Luke might try to kill one or both of us in a fit of rage.

I tried to schedule a visit with Luke, but visits needed approval twenty-four hours in advance. I made an appointment for the next day. The raging storms of my emotions caused another sleepless night. I was utterly exhausted, and no amount of makeup could hide the dark circles plaguing my eyes when I drove to my scheduled appointment. To my dismay, Luke refused to see me.

I tried to visit three more times, but the detention center said Luke didn't want to see me, and they couldn't put me on the visiting roster until he approved my visit. He eventually took a phone call and agreed to let me visit if I'd bring some things he wanted. However, it was evident he had no interest in seeing me. He was just using me to get something he wanted from home. He also knew a hearing was coming up to determine whether he'd be released into my custody.

At the visit, he shuffled across the room, eyes downcast, cracking his knuckles. When I tried to hug him, he pushed me away like I had the plague. Then, giving me half of his attention, we had an amicable talk. I assured him I was praying for him. I also arranged to drop off and pick up some schoolwork so he could get credit and not have to repeat eleventh grade since he'd already refused to go to summer school.

Luke was assigned a probation officer, an empathetic, friendly man. We discussed our options. Luke wanted me to take him home with an ankle monitor. The probation officer explained that if Luke came home, I'd be responsible for him. I, in turn, explained that Luke did whatever he wanted, and there wasn't much I could do to control him.

Luke slouched in the courtroom with his arms across his chest. He refused to look at the judge and was furious when he decided to send him back to juvenile detention. He stopped doing his schoolwork. He refused to let me visit and he wouldn't talk to me on the phone. The probation officer advised Luke that refusing to speak to me made him appear uncooperative, which would make it that much harder to obtain a release. He began communicating again and also resumed his schoolwork.

After several discussions, the judge, probation officer, and I agreed that Luke should go to a rehabilitation facility for three to four months. I wanted him to stop using marijuana and to get help with his major anger issues. When I told Luke, I made it sound like he didn't have a choice. I knew if he found out it was my decision, he'd hate me for it.

Sending my son to rehab was one of the hardest things I'd ever done. I could only hope that the program would work and that he'd eventually recognize I'd done it for his own good. The following day, a van transported Luke to the rehabilitation facility.

I submitted the schoolwork Luke had completed in juvenile detention. He received full credit for the year, which meant he could move on to his senior year and hopefully graduate. When I dropped Luke's work off to his auto body teacher, the teacher gave me a Student of the Month Certificate of Recognition Luke had earned for April right before he'd been arrested. The bittersweet irony of that brought me to tears.

During his first days at the rehab facility, Luke wouldn't talk to me on the phone. He started talking to me only after being told that it would take longer to get released if he didn't cooperate and give the program a chance to work. They also suggested family sessions to figure out what was bothering Luke and learn to work through it.

Mike and I started visiting Luke every Saturday. We assured him we were praying for him and reminded him he could talk to God anytime he wanted. But Luke made little response. I wasn't sure where his faith was by this point, and he hadn't been to church in a year.

I was able to get Luke signed up for summer school at the rehab facility to complete the necessary credits to graduate with his senior class. Since he was taking classes, he didn't have to attend many group sessions and other activities. He was happy about that since he was still extra reserved around others, especially expressing his feelings.

However, Luke began opening up to his counselor and making significant progress. During our first visits, we were in a large room with other kids also visiting parents. Luke said, "Many parents don't visit their kids at all. Maybe some live too far away or don't have the means to get here. But some of the parents have just washed their hands of their kids and given up on them."

"I will never give up on you, and there's nothing you can ever do that will make me stop loving you. Even if you kill me, I'd still love you and forgive you with my dying breath. I assure you that God never gives up on anyone, not these kids whose parents have given up or you either, Luke."

The next weekend, Luke was allowed to leave the facility with us for three hours. He wasn't interested in going out to eat, so we had a pleasant visit at a picnic table in the park. I was astonished at how respectful he seemed. Maybe the rehab counselors were getting through to him.

I began to have hope that all this would work out. God is good. Why did I doubt that God always knows what is best? Jesus once told his disciples: "You do not realize now what I am doing, but later you will understand." (John 13:7) I need to always remember to trust God because he is the only one who sees the whole picture and knows the ending.

In July, Mike's mom Agnes passed away. She'd been a loving grandmother to Luke and a great mother-in-law to me. I called Luke's counselor, and he gave Luke a thirty-six-hour pass to attend the funeral. It was a beautiful memorial. Though we missed her, we were thankful Agnes was no longer in pain since she was in heaven with her Savior.

On our way back to the rehab facility, Luke informed me he didn't believe in God anymore. If he didn't believe in God, I asked, what did he believe?

"I believe in a higher power and life after death. But there is no God."

"It's your right to make your own decision as to what you believe. You know what I taught you when you were younger. But the world speaks for itself. Who but God could have created this beautiful world and all its glory?" I didn't want to get into an argument, so I simply reminded him I'd always be there if he wanted to talk and ended it there.

Luke was released in August. His counselor told me he was among the fastest to complete the program. Luke and I discussed with his teacher how much more work he had to finish to graduate from high school. He chose to rush through the rest of the work rather than return to regular classes. That cost him good grades, but it was a wise choice as he'd have his high school diploma. More important, it was Luke's choice, not mine, and I was very proud of him.

The rehab facility transported Luke to court for his final hearing. I left work around lunchtime to attend. They officially approved his release and sent him home with me. He'd be on probation for several months, have to pass regular drug tests, and meet weekly with his probation officer.

I was so happy to have Luke home. His eyes sparkled in the sunlight and his smile lit up his entire face when he saw his cat, but she was mad at him for being away so long. Now tears replaced his sparkly eyes, and my heart broke for how upset I knew he was. Now that he was home, Luke became distant. He told me numerous times that he couldn't forgive me for sending him away. He said his probation officer had told him I could have taken him home instead and that rehab was my idea.

I doubted the officer had put it like that, as he was a kind man, but I cried most of that night, fearing my son would hate me forever. Mike reminded me we didn't have a choice and were only trying to help him. But no mother wants her son to hate her, and I found it hard to live with myself.

I eventually spent some quality time with Luke when the probation officer permitted me to take him out of state to our time-share in Virginia. Luke was excited to go. He wanted to drive, and I let him do so part of the way. Of course, he enjoyed the whirlpool tub as soon as we got there, which helped put him in a better mood.

The trip proved quite beneficial in repairing our relationship. On the long drive home, we discussed his future. Luke told me he wanted to meet a wonderful girl, fall in love, and have children. He already had their names picked out, Johnny or Frank for a boy and Anna or Alexandra for a girl. That surprised me, but I was so happy to hear him make plans for the future and talk about sharing his life with someone other than his cat and me. Maybe his next step would be getting a job.

A month or so passed. Luke regularly attended his probation visits. I reminded him he needed to stay clean and not fail any drug tests. But it was like talking to a wall. He was drinking again, and he didn't care that he could be arrested for being underage. At least he didn't fail his drug test, which meant he wasn't using marijuana again, one small bit of good news.

Luke was only allowed to use his car to look for a job. He made the excuse that he'd have to tell a prospective employer he was on probation, so he might as well wait until he finished probation. All his friends were in their senior year of high school, which Luke didn't have to attend since he'd already done the coursework for his diploma. I was thankful for that as he still said he hated me for sending him to rehab and told me bluntly he'd have dropped out of school anyway if I tried to make him go back to classes.

Despite his attitude, I sensed it was imperative to spend quality time with Luke. On Wednesdays, I didn't have to be at work until noon, so I'd spend time playing Xbox with him in the morning. I often got called in early, which upset Luke, but that meant he wanted to be with me, so I considered it a win.

Luke was supposed to be released from probation at Thanksgiving, but he failed his drug test. He had to pass three drug tests to get released. In December 2015, he did pass the drug test and was finally released from probation. I was elated, and Luke was relieved. I was hoping he'd get a job now that his probation was complete. But instead of getting better, Luke slept as much as his cat, which was constant, and things were only about to worsen.

24. Does Luke Love Me?

In January 2016, Luke turned eighteen. His dream was to move out on his own, but for that, he'd need an income. He was still unwilling to look for a job. He wouldn't even drop off a résumé or fill out an application. He needed help, but since he wouldn't see a doctor or psychologist, there wasn't much I could do.

Mike and I began feeling we'd be supporting him forever. He started smoking three packs of cigarettes a week. He was again using marijuana heavily. I let him use my credit card for basic needs, which really added up. He did chores around the house, cleaning, cutting the grass, and shoveling the sidewalks. He painted, cleaned, vacuumed, and washed cars for my parents when they needed help.

This earned him a bit of cash but not enough to begin supporting himself. It was again a flashback to Tony partying and earning minimum wage while I worked hard to support our household.

In March, Luke's final probation paperwork was filed. I took him to his favorite restaurant, Chili's, to celebrate. I told him I was proud of him. I also suggested he needed to get a job. I asked him to consider seeing someone about his antisocial issues, and he said he'd think about getting a job but would not go back to counseling.

One afternoon while Mike was at work, I drove Luke to a dental appointment. He needed a filling, and as soon as we were on the road, he asked if the dentist would be using a needle to numb his gums.

"They always do," I reminded him.

"Then I'm not going."

Immediately, my heart started pounding hard. I reminded Luke that the dentist charged for the appointment if clients didn't give a twenty-four-hour notice to cancel, which meant I'd be charged for the visit whether he went or not. Luke started yelling at me. My heart began thumping so hard in my chest I had to pull the car over.

Luke stared at me. "What are you doing?"

I explained that I was having chest pain and trouble breathing. I sat there for a bit, hoping it would stop, but it didn't. "Luke, I need to go to the hospital. Can you please drive me there?"

Luke's expression finally showed some concern. Changing places with me, he began driving to the hospital. My heart was pounding again to the point I was afraid I might die. It felt like a concrete block was sitting on my chest. Pulling into the emergency room parking lot, Luke asked, "How long is this going to take."

"I don't know," I managed to gasp out through my chest pain. "They'll probably have to run some tests."

Luke just looked at me. "I don't like hospitals."

"Fine," I told him, getting out of the car. "Just leave if you don't care about me."

"Fine. Text me when you're finished, and I'll come and pick you up." With that, he drove off.

I made my way into the emergency room, thinking, *My son doesn't even love me enough to go in with me. What if this is it, and I die?* I was petrified. The emergency personnel did an electrocardiogram (ECG), hooked up an IV, ordered blood work and a chest x-ray, and asked all sorts of questions.

After completing the ECG, they assured me it wasn't a heart attack. The doctor eventually came in and told me the tests all looked good. Based on what I'd told him, he concluded I'd experienced an anxiety attack. They released me with the advice to follow up with my primary care physician.

I called Luke to pick me up, but he didn't answer his phone. I sent him a text, then began walking. After about thirty minutes, Luke pulled up alongside me. I climbed into the car and we headed home. He said he hadn't heard his phone because he'd fallen asleep. How could he be sleeping when I could have been dying? He didn't even ask if I was okay.

That confirmed my suspicions that there was something seriously wrong with Luke. Either he didn't love me, or he had some mental issues. I knew he loved me, so it had to be the latter. I forgot to call Mike in all the chaos because I was too upset thinking my son didn't want to be with me while I could have been dying.

That fall, I talked to Luke about getting a job at an auto body shop. His auto body teacher had liked him. Luke called the teacher, who said Luke could use him as a reference. We'd sold the Subaru Impreza we'd paid for out of pocket when Luke backed it into the parked truck. I told Luke I'd get him another car when he got a job.

In the end, Luke decided not to look for a job. When I asked him why, he said he was worried his boss would hover over him, watching every move he made, which in turn might provoke him to yell at his boss and get fired.

What was I to do with my son whom I loved more than anything or anyone else? For now, I needed to support Luke as long as I could. If only he'd be willing to seek professional help, they might be able to diagnose his problem and develop some kind of treatment plan that would help him live a productive life.

For Christmas that year and his nineteenth birthday, Luke asked for money instead of gifts. He wanted to get a place of his own or move in with his friends. I had furniture and other things set aside for when he had his place. But I also worried about him living alone because he showed increasing paranoia. He thought everyone was out to get him. Every time we went for a ride, he insisted people were staring at him.

I'd inherited Tony's .38 Special. Luke began asking me for the gun. I told him no and made sure he couldn't get ahold of it. I prayed God would provide Luke with the help he needed. I didn't know what kind of help that might be as I'd done everything I could without Luke's consent. But I needed to remember that nothing was impossible for God. I'd spent every day of Luke's life praying for his salvation and God's direction for his heart and head.

By spring, Luke still hadn't looked for a job. He was always doing odd jobs for my parents, other people, and me to earn money. But Mike and I were giving up hope he'd ever find a job and be self-supporting. We'd come to terms with that as we both agreed he wasn't capable of taking care of himself. We weren't sure what was wrong, but we knew Luke had major issues.

In April, Luke started hanging out with a new friend I'd met a few times when the young man stopped by our house. A little older than Luke, he seemed friendly. He lived in a nearby town, so it was convenient to drop Luke off at his house or pick him up and bring him to our house. The young man had a minimum wage job and was trying to talk Luke into working with him. I reminded Luke that if he got a job, Mike and I would buy him a car and pay his auto insurance so he could drive back and forth to work. We'd do anything to help him if he was willing to help himself.

In May, I found several painful lumps in my breasts, so I made an appointment with a breast care specialist. She didn't think they were cysts, so she immediately ordered a mammogram and a biopsy. When she mentioned the possibility of cancer, I started crying. She put her hand on my shoulder and smiled confidently. "We will get through this together. I don't want you to worry. We won't know anything until we get the test results."

When I told Mike, he was worried but assured me everything was in God's hands. My anxiety grew, but I reminded myself of Jesus's words in the Sermon on the Mount:

"Therefore do not worry about tomorrow, for tomorrow will worry about itself. Each day has enough trouble of its own." (Matt. 6:34) When I told Luke the doctor was concerned I might have breast cancer, he appeared indifferent. I was hurt, feeling he didn't care. When Mike got home, I told him how Luke had reacted.

Mike assured me Luke cared but didn't know how to show it because he was unable to process his emotions. We both knew Luke loved me. But when he got upset, he held everything inside. He'd acted the same way when he dropped me off at the hospital. I realized Mike was right but wished I knew how to fix mental issues.

The doctor finally called to schedule a different kind of mammogram. Anxiety consumed me as I endured the second mammogram. I texted Luke to express my concern. He texted back, telling me not to worry and that everything would be fine. At least he appeared to care about me now. Finally, the doctor let me know that the new test had been negative and there was nothing to worry about. What a relief! I texted both Luke and Mike to give them the good news.

After all that stress, I needed to relax, so I planned a short vacation at our time-share in Virginia with my mom, sister, and nephews. Luke joined us. Luke asked to drive on the way to the condo. He was speeding. When I told him to slow down crossing the train tracks, he slowed down so much that I was afraid we would get rear-ended. There wasn't any happy medium with Luke's driving; he either drove way too fast or way too slow. That week we watched movies, and he enjoyed spending time in the whirlpool tub. I enjoyed simply spending quality time with him.

When we got home, we found out that Luke's friend had moved to the borough of Old Conemaugh, a rough area with many bars and a high crime rate, about fifteen minutes from our house. I allowed Luke to take my car to visit him, hoping the young man could talk Luke into getting a job. If Luke could just get one job and start earning a paycheck, maybe he'd come out of his shell.

In July, Mike and I vacationed in the Bahamas. When we got home, Luke asked how our vacation had gone. "It was the best trip I've ever taken."

His pleasure showed on his face. "I'm glad to hear that. What all did you do? Did you rent a boat again?"

"No, we spent the whole week sitting on the beach staring at the prettiest water I've ever seen in my life," I responded with a big smile.

I showed Luke all the breathtaking pictures on my phone. He agreed they were gorgeous and said he'd never forget the great experience he'd had there with us.

25. NIGHTMARE

It was just a couple of weeks after that amicable conversation with Luke when I received the knock at the door that is every parent's worst nightmare. I'd just gotten back from work that Wednesday evening, August 2, 2017, when Luke called asking me to pick him up from his friend's place in Old Conemaugh so he could get some stuff from home, then drive him back.

I've already mentioned our discussion, making clear that if I went out again to pick Luke up, that would be it for the night. He'd just have to stay home. But Luke wasn't willing to come home for the night. "It's not a big deal. I'll figure something out. I love you, Mom."

"I love you too."

I'm so thankful we both ended with those words because they were the last words we'd ever say to each other. Instead of Luke coming home eventually, as he'd always done, the terrible ringing of the doorbell roused Mike and me from a dead sleep. The police then gave us the horrible news that another young man had murdered my beloved nineteen-year-old son over a marijuana sale. The information poured over me like a bucket of iced water. Bursting into tears, I struggled to regain my composure. My baby was gone, and I'd never be the same. My core would forever have a gaping hole, a hole Luke once filled. It was slim comfort to know he died instantly and without suffering.

Mike and I didn't even try to go back to sleep. But neither did we want to wake people up with the news in the middle of the night. So we just sat there, sharing tears and hugs but not speaking. What was there to say? That awful feeling of something terrible looming over us had come true. But instead of Luke doing something horrific to us or stepping so far outside the law he got arrested again, he was the victim. And not without some blame. Just like his biological father, my beautiful son's dangerous choices had caught up with him.

At 4:00 a.m. I couldn't wait any longer, so I called my sister Jamie. She put me on speakerphone so her husband could hear as well. They were both distraught at the news and insisted on coming right over. Jamie works in the medical field, and Jerry is a fireman and paramedic, so I thought it would be a good idea for them to be with us when we told my parents, who both had health problems.

A little after 5:00 a.m., the telephone ringing woke my parents from a dead sleep. I told them we were on our way over. The four of us sat with them in the living room while my sister and Jerry told my parents what had happened. They were both crying, and I could feel the depth of their pain. Dad eventually left for a drive, which was what he did when things bothered him. Luke inherited that from Dad because he, too, liked to drive around when he was upset.

When Mike and I got home, he called his family while I called all the Yuzwas. I also texted my pastor. He stopped by a few hours later. "I'm sorry to hear about Luke's murder, Tammy," he said softly with such naked sympathy in his eyes that my chest ached. "Let me know if there is anything I can do for you?" I asked him to officiate Luke's funeral service. He also arranged for special music from our church worship director. We set the memorial service for 11:00 a.m., Monday, August 7, at my mom's church since ours was booked for the date. I'd decided on cremation, just like Luke's father, Tony.

By this point, I was learning more details of Luke's last moments. Around 9:30 p.m., twenty-two-year-old Tyrone McDuffie of Johnstown had come by the house where Luke was staying with his friend to purchase marijuana brownies and THC capsules, which I eventually found out Luke had been producing. After getting into an argument with Luke, Tyrone used a semiautomatic firearm to shoot Luke in the head, then grabbed Luke's backpack containing the marijuana products and ran off.

Two friends who were with Luke when he was shot immediately called 911. They told the police the name of the shooter and were willing to testify. I have the utmost respect for both of them for courageously putting their lives on the line to speak up. Unfortunately, the 911 dispatcher told them to go back and check if Luke was still breathing.

I can't imagine the anguish that must have been for them, shaking so badly it would be hard to feel a pulse, seeing Luke's blood all around him, the lifelessness of his body sprawled on the cold ground. My heart broke for them because they must be hurting over the loss of their friend and would have to live with those images for the rest of their lives. I wanted to reach out to comfort them. To let them know I was praying for them. To let them know God loved them, and so did I.

I was relieved they hadn't tried to attack the shooter. As Luke's mother, I have no question if someone shot my son in front of me, I'd have gone after the shooter and tried to retrieve the gun. But if they'd tried to do that, I'm sure they would have been shot too. They did the right thing by just calling 911.

Thanks to their quick reporting, the police caught Luke's murderer within a half hour of the shooting. He had a lengthy criminal history and had already spent two years in state prison. A test for gunshot residue on him came back positive, and a video surveillance camera in the neighborhood had caught him leaving the scene.

Late one evening, several days after Luke's death, Mike and I were sitting on the porch when a car pulled into our driveway. A young man got out of the car, walked up to the porch, and introduced himself as the friend who drove Luke home, then back to Old Conemaugh the night of Luke's death. He expressed how deeply sorry he was for what had happened.

He went on to explain that Luke had come home that evening to get his cell phone charger and twelve hundred dollars he'd saved to purchase a gun, which had been prearranged for that night. Luke had told him he didn't feel safe. Since I'd refused to give him Tony's gun, he'd made arrangements to buy his own.

At least now I knew the reason for such a senseless shooting. Tyrone had known Luke had the gun money on him and shot him to steal it. It might seem strange to others, but I found so much peace in Luke's friend giving me these details. At least I wouldn't have to spend the rest of my life trying to figure out what happened. I also appreciated that he'd been there for my son because Luke wasn't easy to befriend.

That weekend, I once again tried calling the last number Luke called me from. This time, Luke's friend answered. He started crying and telling me over and over how sorry he was. He apologized for not doing anything to stop the shooter. I assured him he'd done the right thing and that I didn't blame him. After all, there wasn't anything he could have done to help Luke at that point.

I posted a message on Facebook for Luke's few friends I could reach that way. I asked them to please share the post to get the word out of Luke's passing. It read:

R.I.P., Luke J. Yuzwa, my only child by blood. I was blessed to have Luke in my life for the nineteen years God loaned him to me. Now he is back with his Creator and at peace. He has no more pain, sorrows, or worries. Although I will miss him, others are now holding him in their arms for a joyful reunion. Thank you, Father, for giving Luke to me. He's yours, God, not mine. You loved him before I knew him, and he belongs to you. Be with him now that I can't. Amen. Luke, Kayley and I will see you again one day.

In all of this, I felt like Job, the biblical patriarch from the land of Uz whose story is told in the Old Testament book by that name. A righteous, God-fearing man, Job had been blessed by God with great wealth, vast herds of livestock, twelve children, and a wife. The devil challenged God that Job was only good because God had blessed him so much and that Job would curse God if he lost those blessings. God allowed the devil to test Job. In one day, Job lost all his children and riches. But instead of losing his faith or cursing God, he bowed down in worship, saying:

"Naked I came from my mother's womb, and naked I will depart. The Lord gave and the Lord has taken away; may the name of the Lord be praised." (Job 1:21)

I hadn't lost everything. But I'd lost my only son, the most important person in my life, and it felt as though the world was caving in around me. Thankfully, true peace doesn't depend on our circumstances but in surrendering our circumstances to a loving heavenly Father, as Jesus reminded his disciples right before going to the cross:

"Peace I leave with you; my peace I give you. I do not give to you as the world gives. Do not let your hearts be troubled and do not be afraid." (John 14:27)

I prayed that I could be as strong in my faith as Job. But did I need to forgive Tyrone? Do you think God wants us to forgive everyone, or do people need to meet certain conditions before forgiving them? Here are the Bible verses I used to make my decision:

"And when you stand praying, if you hold anything against anyone, forgive them, so that your Father in heaven may forgive you your sins." (Mark 11:25)

"Be kind and compassionate to one another, forgiving each other, just as in Christ God forgave you." (Eph. 4:32)

Luke 23:26–43 says:

As the soldiers led him away, they seized Simon from Cyrene, who was on his way in from the country, and put the cross on him and made him carry it behind Jesus. A large number of people followed him, including women who mourned and wailed for him. Jesus turned and said to them, "Daughters of Jerusalem, do not weep for me; weep for yourselves and for your children. For the time will come when you will say, 'Blessed are the childless women, the wombs that never bore and the breasts that never nursed!' Then "'they will say to the mountains, "Fall on us!" and to the hills, "Cover us!"' For if people do these things when the tree is green, what will happen when it is dry?"

Two other men, both criminals, were also led out with him to be executed. When they came to the place called the Skull, they crucified him there, along with the criminals—one on his right, the other on his left. Jesus said, "Father, forgive them, for they do not know what they are doing." And they divided up his clothes by casting lots.

The people stood watching, and the rulers even sneered at him. They said, "He saved others; let him save himself if he is God's Messiah, the Chosen One."

The soldiers also came up and mocked him. They offered him wine vinegar and said, "If you are the king of the Jews, save yourself."

There was a written notice above him, which read: THIS IS THE KING OF THE JEWS.

One of the criminals who hung there hurled insults at him: "Aren't you the Messiah? Save yourself and us!"

But the other criminal rebuked him. "Don't you fear God," he said, "since you are under the same sentence? We are punished justly, for we are getting what our deeds deserve. But this man has done nothing wrong."

Then he said, "Jesus, remember me when you come into your kingdom."

Jesus answered him, "Truly I tell you, today you will be with me in paradise."

I love that passage from Luke. Even while Jesus was hanging on the cross, he prayed to his father: "Father, forgive them, for they do not know what they are doing." I can't think of anything worse that can happen than the death of a loved one. While Jesus was suffering terribly on the cross, he had a big enough heart to think about the forgiveness of those hurting him.

Forgiveness is like an anchored ship. You need to lift the anchor before you can start moving in any direction or change direction. You cannot steer a ship with the anchor in place, but it becomes effortless to steer the ship once you lift the anchor.

In the same way, in order to forgive, you need to choose to forgive. Choosing to forgive is a willful act in your mind. Start by listing in your mind what needs to be forgiven. How did someone offend you? Was it in a relationship? Maybe it was something someone said or did. Keeping Matthew 6:14–15 in mind that God will only forgive you *if* you forgive others will help you decide to forgive. Then pray to God and surrender this person's action to him. Release control over the situation to God. That's forgiveness. Forgiveness does not mean that you judge them and decide if their action is right or wrong. Only after handing everything over to God can you start to move past the hurt that this person has caused you.

It will take time to forget what they did, or you may never forget, but you need to move past it. You don't have to restore your relationship with this person. Allow God to direct you if that needs to happen because it is his will. But if you first don't ever choose to forgive them, you will never accomplish this.

One final piece of advice: don't hold on to bitterness. Instead, every time it comes into your mind, surrender it to God. As you do this, it will enter your mind less often. You may need to forgive this person daily. It may not be a one-time thing, but if you truly commit to fully surrendering everything to God, his grace will replace your bitterness. You don't have to trust someone to forgive them. You only need to trust God with your pain.

1 Peter 3:9 says not to repay evil with evil. That verse clearly told me what I needed to do.

After a lot of praying, I was able to forgive Tyrone for killing my only child. Having been forgiven of so much, how could I not forgive my son's killer? That doesn't mean I didn't want justice for my only child's murder. Only God could have given me the strength to forgive. I prayed that God would show me his purpose and plan for allowing all this to happen. God is sovereign. As Scripture reminds us:

"For my [God's] thoughts are not your thoughts, neither are your ways my ways," declares the Lord. "As the heavens are higher than the earth, so are my ways higher than your ways and my thoughts than your thoughts." (Isa. 55:8–9)

Like Job, I might not understand why God was doing what he was doing. But God created my son and me, and God has the right to do whatever he sees fit with our lives. So God either caused Luke to be taken from this earth, allowed it to happen, or could have prevented it from happening.

Because I already knew the outcome, I knew God had allowed this to happen as he certainly didn't choose to let someone else be shot or prevent it from happening altogether. Therefore, I had complete faith that God is always in control and will keep his promise to work even terrible circumstances for my good:

"And we know that in all things God works for the good of those who love him, who have been called according to his purpose." (Rom. 8:28)

I will always wonder, until I'm in heaven and can ask my heavenly Father face-to-face, why God chose to allow Luke's death rather than all the things I'd prayed for my son. But until then, I've decided to trust him completely and follow wherever he leads me. What more can I say than what Jesus taught us to pray and prayed himself in the garden of Gethsemane: "Thy will be done." (Matt. 6:10; Luke 22:42)

26. Eulogy

That weekend, something extraordinary happened when Mike and I attended a Saturday evening service at our church. While we were singing, I saw a vision. There is no other word to describe it. As clear as day, in my mind I saw Luke in the sky. He was singing, his arms raised in worship and a big smile on his face. He looked so happy. It reminded me of the times when I was sad and he used to tell me jokes to cheer me up. If only I could see his face again and hold him in my arms one last time.

My dad later told me he'd had a similar vision just the day before. It was such a wonderful experience that God would choose to provide this comfort to us. It confirmed to me that Luke was in heaven.

During the Sunday morning worship service the next day, our pastor called Mike and me up to the stage. He explained to the congregation what had happened, then prayed for us. When he finished, I asked the congregation to pray that God would speak to Tyrone's heart and let him know he is loved.

The following morning in my house's cold quiet, the icy dread of Luke's impending memorial service enveloped me. I was a bundle of nerves over giving Luke's eulogy. Nevertheless, I refused to let myself cry as we drove to my mom's church. Some of the church women had provided refreshments and would take care of the cleanup. I was grateful to see many of Luke's friends among the guests. They tried awkwardly to comfort me, but I ended up comforting them instead.

The pastor gave a brief message. Then our church's worship director sang a song I'd requested, "Oceans Where Feet May Fail," written by the Christian music group Hillsong United. The lyrics speak of resting in God's embrace and keeping our eyes above the waves and on our Savior even when we're sinking into the deepest, stormiest oceans.

As the beautiful lyrics rang out, I began shaking so badly I whispered to Mike and my sister Jamie that I didn't think I'd be able to speak. All I could think of was that I'd never get to see my precious son again. Even clasping my hands tightly together couldn't stop the shaking.

I prayed for God to give me strength, and he did. Suddenly, I was singing along with the worship director. The louder I sang, the stronger I became until most of the shaking subsided. Now I could get up in front of everyone, including Luke's friends, and present God's message of love, forgiveness, and salvation as I knew God was calling me to do.

I started Luke's eulogy by thanking all who'd come and shared some of Luke's most endearing qualities and favorite things. Then I shifted to the message God had laid on my heart.

"God has given me such peace. Otherwise, I would not be able to stand up here. The Bible says we all live once, die once, and after that, we face judgment over what we've done with our lives (Heb. 9:27). What that means is we're all on a journey called life, headed to a destination we can't get to until we cross to the other side. That's what we call death.

"The question is, where will we spend the rest of eternity once we reach the other side? Will we spend eternity in heaven with our Lord and Savior Jesus Christ, or will we spend it apart from our Lord? I know where I'm going to spend eternity, and I pray that you do too. If you died tonight and had to stand before God, why should he let you into heaven? If your answer is because you are a good person, the Bible says none are good enough and we all have sinned. We can't find salvation through our good works, and we can't work our way into heaven. It's only through believing in Jesus that we are saved. He loved us so much that he died for us on the cross. I know Luke is in heaven because he accepted Jesus as his Lord and Savior when he was seven years old."

Looking down at my notes, my throat burned from holding back my tears, like a dam stopping a flood. I blinked as if dust got in my eyes. Jamie asked if she should take over, but I took a deep breath and told her I'd be fine. Then I went on.

"Tomorrow is not promised to any of us. Life is fleeting and fragile, and it may be gone in an instant. We never know when our time here on earth will run out. That's why we must be ready. Don't put off asking Jesus to come into your heart as Lord and Savior, thinking you can always do it tomorrow."

Glancing toward heaven, I continued. "Bottom line, you never know if you will have a tomorrow. Sometimes death comes slowly, and people have time to think about death and what will happen after they die. But others are taken suddenly and tragically with no time to prepare for death. Just think of Luke. He was simply walking down the street with no warning that he was about to take his last breath."

As at my grandmother's funeral, I read Henry van Dyke's powerful poem about death from the *Our Daily Bread* devotional titled "A Sailing Ship." Then I went on.

"I hope you find comfort in this beautiful description of homecoming to heaven. I know I do when I think of meeting my Savior and all my friends and family who've gone on before me, including my precious son Luke. I pray that in remembrance of Luke, you will each take this opportunity to prepare for that eternal life today if you haven't already."

When I finished, I was once again shaking uncontrollably, but I made it back to my seat. The pastor picked up where I left off in presenting the gospel message, and several people did accept Jesus Christ into their hearts that day. So many people approached me afterward to say what a powerful impact Luke's eulogy had on them. It was all for God's glory, and without his strength, it wouldn't have happened.

Mike told me I was amazing and how proud he was of me. He'd been worried when the song started because I was shaking so hard. But as I began singing louder and louder with the worship director, he knew that nothing was going to stop me. I usually sing quietly since I have a terrible singing voice. So that, too, was a miracle.

I can't wait until the day comes when I meet my heavenly Father face-to-face and all of my loved ones who have passed on to heaven before me. Meanwhile, until God calls me home, I will continue to love the unlovable and forgive the unforgivable—including my son's killer. I will tell everyone I can of God's immeasurable love, grace, mercy, and forgiveness.

27. God's Comfort

When we arrived home from Luke's funeral, I opened the mail as I always do before dinner. My heart seemed to stop beating when I saw Luke's death certificate. Through my tears, I read every word, including Tony's name as Luke's father. My heart broke again for all the moments Luke had lost with his dad.

The time of death was given as 10:56 p.m. even though Luke had died just after 9:30 p.m. The immediate cause of death was listed as a gunshot wound to the head. I began hyperventilating. No parent should have to hold their child's death certificate in their hands. I prayed for God to give me strength as I still had to face the murder trial, and I felt I couldn't go on.

The preliminary hearing for Luke's murder was set for September 8, 2017. The assistant district attorney had let us know family could attend. I arrived at the courthouse with my mom and brother-in-law Jerry. Whispering to his lawyer, Tyrone's large calloused hand pointed at us in a gesture of defiance. My blood boiled, and I couldn't control the heat emanating from my body as his narrowed eyes angrily stared at us. Tyrone didn't look away when I stared back; it was as if he didn't care. We stared at each other for a long moment—so long that my eyes were dry from not blinking. When the ADA stated the charges against him, he finally turned away. His attorney asked for a continuance, and a second hearing was set for September 22. And with that, it was over.

Returning to the room where we'd been waiting to be called into the courtroom, I asked if I could speak to Luke's two friends who'd been with Luke when he was shot. They were there that day in case they got called to testify. They came in, crying and telling me how sorry they were. I hugged them both, reassuring them they couldn't have done anything more than they had in the circumstances, and told them to keep in touch if they ever needed to talk. They were so surprised I was comforting them instead of the other way around.

That said, I was really struggling with my loss. I missed Luke terribly. I was distraught that his killer's arraignment had been postponed after all our effort to be there, and the last thing I wanted was to go back for a second hearing.

I finally decided the only way I'd be able to stop myself from attending the second hearing was if I physically could not get there. A trip to Iceland had been on my bucket list, and since I had faith Luke was in heaven, I figured I'd feel close to him if I could see the northern lights (aurora borealis) in the heavens. Unfortunately, Mike had to work, and I couldn't find anyone interested in going with me, so I booked a solo trip to Reykjavik.

I was at my gate waiting to board when a young man around my son's age started chatting with me. His name was Joseph. I told him this was my first trip to Iceland. He asked if I knew anything about the Golden Circle. This must-see consists of Iceland's three most popular tourist attractions: Gullfoss Waterfall, Geysir Geothermal Area, and Thingvellir National Park. I told him I was planning to go there. He said he'd reserved a rental car to drive there. I asked if he'd like company for the drive. We agreed to meet up when we landed.

I wasn't sure he'd be waiting when I got off the plane. I didn't want to impose, but I was nervous about traveling alone, so it would be a blessing if we could ride together. It might sound a bit crazy to feel safer with a stranger than being alone in Iceland. But I've always been a bit too trusting, as Mike would undoubtedly agree, and in this case, it certainly turned out for the best.

I walked straight through baggage claim since I only had carry-on luggage. Joseph didn't have any checked bags either, as he'd mentioned having only a backpack. I spotted him sitting on a bench. He called out for me. Heading over, I asked if he still wanted to travel together.

He did, so we picked up his rental car, then headed to a small apartment I'd booked in Reykjavik for the first four nights, as that had proved far cheaper than a hotel. It had a full kitchen, so I figured I'd save money by cooking as well. We both took time to shower since we'd spent the night on a plane. Within the hour, we headed to the Golden Circle.

The drive through Iceland's splendor is one of a kind. The day was sunny at first. Then a sheet of rain could be seen in the distance. I could hear its roar. The cars faded behind the mist until I could see them no more. Then came a torrential downpour followed by hail. But neither of us let the weather ruin our trip. We saw geysers, lava rocks, caves, and a massive waterfall.

The rain finally stopped while we were at the waterfall. A beautiful rainbow appeared above it. Right then, I could feel Luke's presence. It was such a blessing from God as though God showed me that he is always with me, and so is Luke. Through the roar of the waterfall, I could hear God whispering to my heart, "Trust me." I had a hard time saying goodbye to Joseph when he dropped me off at my apartment that night.

The next day, I did a northern lights tour with a guide named Siggi, who used equipment to track the lights. I was on top of the world, literally. Siggi parked the SUV. Then the sky started dancing with colorful ribbons of light that got brighter and brighter. I ran over and hugged Siggi. I'd told him earlier about Luke.

"I think Luke must have talked to God and asked for a spectacular show. This is magnificent."

Tears streamed down my cheeks in pure joy over God's goodness in blessing me with such an out-of-this-world experience. Maybe God had allowed Luke to design this show just for me.

I spent my final four days in Iceland at a hotel out in the country. When I arrived, I walked over to take pictures of the Blue Lagoon, a famous spa in Iceland. As I was leaving, a woman and her son, a youth about Luke's age, walked in. I completely lost it. I cried hysterically. The other guests probably thought I was crazy, but I couldn't help it. I would never again have the chance to walk like that with my son. He was gone, and there was nothing I could do to change that.

I'd never felt more alone than at that moment. What was I doing at the top of the world all by myself? I reminded myself that I wasn't alone. God was with me just as the Bible promises:

"He [God] will never leave you nor forsake you." (Deut. 31:6)

I flew home from Iceland determined to go back someday. Yet, even after I was home, God continued blessing me with reminders of my son. One day while meditating to clear my mind, I felt Luke's arms wrap around me and hold me tight. It was such a good feeling that I was in high spirits for the rest of the day.

I'd been praying for God to tell me clearly that Luke is in heaven. God did more than I could have ever asked or imagined. He sent me a dream. In the dream, Luke told me he was in heaven. God knew if I heard it directly from Luke, that would bring me his peace that surpasses all understanding (Phil. 4:7), so that is what he did. I wished I could have stayed there with Luke in the dream. Why did I have to wake up?

In November, I had another dream in which Luke asked me, "How is it that you are crying?"

He didn't ask *why* I was crying but *how*. Meaning there was no reason for me to cry. The only way there'd be no reason for me to cry was if Luke is definitely in heaven. Or maybe it's because there isn't any crying in heaven, so Luke was wondering how I could cry because he can't, being in heaven. Either way, this gave me much comfort when I still struggled with worry about Luke's final home.

My first Christmas without Luke was terrible. I didn't feel like celebrating. Every smile I saw on someone's face reminded me I'd never see Luke smile again here on this earth. He wouldn't be here to celebrate any of our special days together. He'd never be there to comfort me when I was sad or depressed.

Even when I had a moment of happiness, I also felt sadness about feeling happy because Luke wasn't there to share it with me. I didn't want to stop remembering him because then he wouldn't be with me anymore. Yet, at the same time, the constant pain of remembering my loss was like a sword continuously piercing my heart. I would relive the moment he died, wondering if he had even a second or two to see it coming and what he thought of if he did. Did he think of me, his mother who loved him more than anything in the world? I know I'd have been thinking of him.

What made it worse was the feeling that I thought of my son every moment of my life and couldn't forget him, but it seemed at times that all of the rest of the world had. It was as though I had to keep reminding them Luke ever existed. That was my first Christmas without my son.

January 24, 2018, was his first birthday without being with me. So I put the following post on Facebook to honor Luke. It expressed how I felt the day he didn't turn twenty here on this earth and celebrate with me.

Luke Yuzwa, Happy twentieth birthday, I wish. R.I.P. You will never be loved by anyone more than I loved you. You... had so many endearing qualities. Your friends told me that you were always there for them. You didn't like anyone to be sad, so you always tried to cheer everyone up. You were generous, and you were a loyal friend. Thank you all for sharing what a good friend Luke was to you. It makes me proud to have been his mom. Luke, I know you are in heaven where there is only love and happiness, but I so long to be with you... Please be ready for me and greet me with open arms as soon as that time finally comes. Until then, you took a part of my heart with you, so please keep it close. I LOVE YOU, Luke Jacob Yuzwa.

28. PRESERVING MEMORIES

As the months passed, I tried to hide my sadness from Mike, who was always kind, loving, and patient. But with my depression and constant thinking about Luke, I was ignoring the other great love of my life, my amazing husband. So I wanted to do something special for Valentine's Day to show Mike how much I loved him.

Going to his workplace, I put roses on his truck, just as I had for his birthday when we were still dating. I selected three different colors with one rose for every year we'd been together. Mike was very touched. I am so thankful for my husband. God made him perfect and just for me.

Shortly after that, I had another dream of Luke. This time Mike was there as well. Luke sat on my hope chest in our bedroom as vivid as when he was alive. Mike perched on the loveseat while I sat cross-legged on the bed. Looking over at Mike, I gave a nod toward Luke and asked if Mike saw him too.

"Yes, I see him," Mike responded, so I didn't imagine my son's presence. But, of course being a dream, I didn't realize I was dreaming.

Then Luke looked at me. "I'll be in heaven when you die."

"You are there now," I responded.

I think Luke was trying to tell me he's in heaven, and when I die, he'll be there waiting for me. So, God once again comforted me by sending that dream. But, how long would I need to be comforted? Would I ever feel secure enough of Luke's salvation I wouldn't need further reassurance?

Despite those pleasant dreams, my pain was unbearable. Luke's murder had gouged a giant hole in my heart. There is no other way to describe it. I saw Luke's face every time I closed my eyes, but I wanted to be able to touch him. To trace the lines of his face with my fingers. I needed that physical connection.

On Mother's Day weekend, another painful first without him, I decided to arrange some photos of Luke for our family room walls. On two walls, I hung various pictures showing his growth throughout the years. In addition, I had three other treasured portraits I sensed God inspired me to group. Luke as a baby, so sweet and innocent. Another showed how he looked at nineteen, not long before I lost him. The last one depicted Luke in heaven with wings, healthy and happy, symbolizing his resurrection and rebirth. Looking at these pictures gave me a warm feeling that calmed my soul, bringing comfort and peace.

But I also wanted a more permanent reminder of Luke. I've never been a big fan of tattoos and worried about the pain from the tattoo needle. However, one place had an opening that evening, so I made the appointment before losing my courage. I chose Luke's name in his handwriting with his date of death and a heart. The needle did indeed hurt, but the tattoo is a beautiful physical reminder of Luke that is always with me.

Jury selection for Luke's murder was supposed to begin in August 2018. Instead, the ADA called to inform me they were adding new charges against Tyrone for an attempt to solicit drugs from inside prison. Tyrone had tried to get his girlfriend to send him synthetic marijuana. He planned to sell the drugs in prison to get money for attorney fees and other needs.

Tyrone was considering a plea deal. This would mean we wouldn't have to go to trial and that Tyrone would publicly admit he killed Luke. The ADA wanted to know my thoughts on a fair plea deal. Since I'd never been in such a situation, I had no idea, so I deferred it back to her. She believed an offer of forty to eighty years with no chance of parole would be reasonable, so I agreed.

The ADA also thought that hearing the words come out of Tyrone's mouth admitting he'd shot my son would help give me some closure. But there were no words from him that could make any difference to me. I'd already completely forgiven Tyrone. Nothing he said or did could take that peace away from me. While it would always hurt that I no longer had my only child with me, I'd never heal if I gave in to bitterness or resentment.

In the gospel of Matthew, when one of Jesus's disciples, Judas, led the soldiers to arrest him, Jesus responded to Judas's betrayal by calling him "friend" (Matt. 26:47–50). Though Judas was a malicious traitor, Jesus still loved him just as I'd chosen to love Luke's killer. Among Jesus's last words on the cross were:

"Father, forgive them, for they do not know what they are doing." (Luke 23:34) God loves everyone unconditionally. He died for each and every one of us.

I missed Luke so much that many days I longed just to leave this earth and be with my son in heaven. The one thing that kept me from being tempted to commit suicide was knowing that God made me for a purpose. And I had full assurance that my purpose was to love as Jesus did. To show God's love to Luke's betrayer as well as Luke's friends and others. If I took my own life, there would be no one to accomplish that purpose. As the Bible makes clear, we are to love others, not because people always deserve it, but because God first loved us:

"Very rarely will anyone die for a righteous person, though for a good person someone might possibly dare to die. But God demonstrates his own love for us in this: While we were still sinners, Christ died for us." (Rom. 5:7–8)

"This is love: not that we loved God, but that he loved us and sent his Son as an atoning sacrifice for our sins. Dear friends, since God so loved us, we also ought to love one another.... We love because he first loved us." (1 John 4:10–11, 19)

When we love people and don't give up on them, we remember what our Lord and Savior did for us. Sometimes people are hard to love, but the truth is that the people who are the most difficult to love are the ones who need love the most.

August 2, 2018, was the first anniversary of Luke's death. I placed a memorial ad in our local newspaper and put the same post on Facebook as a remembrance of Luke.

One of Luke's friends bought orange balloons for us to release into the sky as a symbolic statement against gun violence. The evening sun glared off the car windows. Not a cloud was visible in the sky when we released the balloons. We watched them float far into the atmosphere. It was a memorable evening, and I didn't break down in tears until 9:34 p.m., the time Luke died.

In all this time, I took care of Luke's cat, Kayley. This was bittersweet as Luke had loved her more than anyone on this earth except perhaps me. Kayley missed Luke as much as I did. Just as she'd done while Luke was away at rehab, any time someone opened the door to enter Luke's room, she'd run up the stairs to see if it was Luke.

Just over a year after Luke's passing, Kayley got sick. The vet couldn't do anything to help her. Since we didn't want her to endure drawn-out suffering, we made the difficult decision to have her put down. The last night with Kayley was torture. Those moments were so precious to me. I finally went to bed but kept getting up during the night to check on her. When I got up in the morning, I held her and cried until it was time to leave the house. Mike brought the carrier up, put her in it, and carried her to the kitchen door. I put her in the back seat of the car; I told her that everything would be okay.

Crying hysterically by then, I kept telling Kayley repeatedly that she was going to see Luke. I didn't know how else to comfort her or myself. If Luke wasn't already in heaven missing his cat, I was sure that I would not have been able to do that. I was so jealous because she would get to see Luke, and I wouldn't. I wanted it to be me, not Kayley that was going to heaven.

When we got to the vet, I carried her in and shielded her eyes from all the dogs. I knew how much she hated dogs. Ever since she was a kitten on the farm where she was born, she was afraid of dogs, understandably so. They took us to a private room right away, probably because I was disturbing the whole waiting room with my loud sobbing. I couldn't help it. It was just unbearable! I felt like Luke was dying all over again because I knew he loved his cat.

About five minutes after we were in the room, the veterinarian came in. He said he had to give her a sedative to keep her calm to find a vein to inject her with the euthanasia solution. I wanted to hold her the whole time because I didn't want her to think we were abandoning her. I didn't care about the pain I was enduring knowing what was happening to her. She was more important than me at that moment, so I held onto her. I felt like she was Luke—like I had to say goodbye to Luke all over again. She was the last piece of my son, and I must willingly hand Kayley over to God! I cried and cried, and I thought she must have known something was wrong. Animals can sense these things. The vet said he had to take her into the other room to give her the sedative. I wasn't happy about that, but I agreed.

He brought her back after about ten minutes. He said she would probably get sleepy and that her head would start falling. He also noted that some animals get angry. I held her tight and supported her head. She wrapped her paws around my shoulders and my neck like she did before. *She was hugging me!* When Luke was a toddler, he used to wrap his arms around my neck and play with my hair. I held Kayley tighter and cried harder. She was not getting drowsy. Then she started to growl at me. She tried to attack me, just like Luke did when he rebelled because I didn't get him released into my custody from juvenile detention. I had no choice but to put Kayley back in her carrier, just like I had to put Luke in rehab. I think Kayley thought that, after the vet brought her back, we would leave, so she gladly jumped into my arms. The longer we stood there, the more she realized that something was wrong because we weren't leaving, so she got angry with me.

After a while, the vet returned and said he would have to give her another shot since he wasn't sure he got the first shot into her. I let him retake her. When he came back with her, I did not try to pick her up. She was very drowsy and appeared to be sleeping with her eyes open. That freaked me out! Was Luke lying on the ground with his eyes open? Who closed them for him if they were open? Oh, the unbearable pain I felt! I bravely rubbed Kayley's cheeks and paws until he said he was ready to inject her. The anguish of that moment was more than I could bear. The vet assured me she was feeling no pain and since I wasn't able to hold her, we decided to leave.

Mike and I left in tears through the back door. I cried most of the day and refused to go to church that night. Sadness overwhelmed me. But as I said before, if Luke wouldn't have already been in heaven waiting for his cat, I could never have done it. I tried to think of it as my last gift to him. Since I couldn't say goodbye to Luke in person, I was sending him his cat—one last gift until the day I see him again when this world ends, or I die. Some people don't believe animals go to heaven, but I do because Isaiah 11:6 describes animals in heaven. I need to think animals go to heaven even though they don't have souls, so I will hold on to my hope until I get to heaven to see for myself. Oh, what a joyous day that will be! I can't wait! I want to see all of my loved ones in heaven. It can't come soon enough. The next few months would be hard because Kayley was always with me. Will I ever stop looking for Kayley every time I walk through the door?

29. JUSTICE

In September, Tyrone turned down the plea deal of forty to eighty years. His public defender had countered with an offer of twenty to forty years. So the ADA suggested we counter with another offer.

The prosecution had two eyewitnesses and a surveillance video of the shooting. Although at a distance, the video clearly showed Tyrone when he passed by the camera since he looked right into it. Plus, there was a positive gun residue test. This was someone's life Tyrone had taken, and we were negotiating his penalty like some real estate deal. Unbelievable.

I was done with the games and wanted to go to trial. The ADA was still pushing for a plea deal because that would mean less chance of an appeal. They didn't want to take any chances of the sentence getting overturned. I understood their reasoning, but I was upset as I wanted closure after more than a year of this dragging out. I reminded myself that everything was in God's timing and held on to prophet Jeremiah's declaration when he was facing difficult trials:

"The Lord is good to those whose hope is in him, to the one who seeks him." (Lam. 3:25)

After several more negotiations, the ADA contacted me in early December 2018. They wanted to know if I'd agree to a plea deal of thirty to sixty years. In my opinion, anything less than life without parole was unfair, but I also knew it wasn't really up to me since the DA's office, not me, would make the final decision. Asking for my input was simply a courtesy to the victim's family.

In the end, I agreed to the plea deal, as did the defense. A few days later, I received a call informing me that Wednesday, December 12, 2018, would be the date for Tyrone's sentencing. I would have the opportunity to present a victim's impact statement during the sentencing.

This was all happening right before Christmas. I was emotionally distraught and cried so much that I was having a hard time functioning at work. I originally prepared just three short, simple points for my impact statement. But God had other plans. On the morning of the sentencing, I listened to a daily devotion from Saddleback Church (drivetimedevot ions.com) as I did every morning. God never fails to speak if we listen for his voice. By the end of the short broadcast, it couldn't have been clearer what God wanted me to say to Tyrone.

Mike, my mom, my sister Jamie and her husband Jerry, and a couple of Luke's friends accompanied me to the sentencing. My stomach lurched with nervousness as we arrived at the courthouse, but I was also energized that this would finally be over.

As we were escorted to our seats in the courtroom, I spotted Tyrone seated at the defense table with his public defender. He was reading some legal documents, and it seemed odd that he wasn't wearing any handcuffs. If he was a dangerous killer, why wasn't he in handcuffs? I reminded myself that God was with me and that one of the most repeated commands in the Bible is to "fear not."

Everyone stood as the judge entered the courtroom. After we were all seated, the judge read off the charges against Tyrone, including criminal homicide and robbery. I was so emotional I couldn't stop shaking. Just then I noticed that no one was on the defense side of the courtroom. Not a single member of his family had shown up to support Tyrone.

With that sad realization, a love only God could give overwhelmed me for this young man. It was so intense I felt my heart was going to burst. I wanted to sit on his side of the courtroom so that he wouldn't be alone.

About ten minutes later, my shaky legs barely got me to the front of the courtroom to give my victim impact statement. I waited to see if Tyrone would look at me. He didn't, so I began.

"Tyrone, when I was listening to a devotional program this morning, God laid on my heart what he wanted me to say to you today. It was a Christmas-themed devotional, and the word for today was *love*. So I'm going to share that devotion with you."

For the first time, Tyrone glanced at me. I went on, "If I asked you to summarize Christmas in one word, you might say *giving* or *joy* or *family*, maybe even *hope*. But the essence of Christmas at its very core is about love. L-O-V-E." I spelled out the individual letters. "In fact, maybe the most well-known verse in the Bible is John 3:16, 'For God so loved the world that he gave his only begotten son, that whoever believes in him should not perish but have everlasting life.'"

Praise God. I now had Tyrone's full attention. "That's it. Christmas is all about love. The love of God who was willing to step into the brokenness, messiness, and sinfulness of humanity and redeem us to himself. Just think about the depth of God's love for you by answering this question. If you knew your son was about to die unjustly because of something someone else had done and it was within your power to prevent his death, wouldn't you stop it from happening?"

Was I getting through to Tyrone? I prayed for God to speak to his heart as I continued, "Of course, you would because you love your son. Imagine then how much God must love you that he would give his only begotten Son to take your place and die for you even when you were sinning against him. The Bible says while we were sinners, Christ died for us. It may not seem to make sense that God would love you and me so deeply. But it's true. The manger shows it. The cross proves it. We worship the only God who loves sinners. He loves the world even when we are sinning against him, and he wants us to love others even when they sin against us."

I finished reading the devotional, then looked directly into Tyrone's soul. "Tyrone, because I am a follower of Jesus, I am required to forgive you. And I have forgiven you from the moment you took my son's life from this earth. I want you to know that God will also forgive you if you ask him. The Bible says that if we confess our sins, he is faithful and just to forgive us. But the Bible also says we reap what we sow. I believe thirty years is too short of a sentence for taking my son's life. But in those thirty years, God is also giving you a chance to find him. And maybe someday you will feel the need to let me know why you decided to kill my son Luke."

Shakily, I rushed back to my seat. Now it was Tyrone's turn to agree to the charges. I tuned everything out, feeling vulnerable and crying a little. At one point, the judge asked Tyrone if he wanted to say anything.

"No." But just as the judge started speaking again, he looked at me and interrupted her. "Your Honor, I do have something I would like to say."

"Do you want to speak to council first?"

"No."

"Then go ahead."

Tyrone turned and addressed me directly. "Like you said before, I don't have any children, so I can't really begin to imagine what you feel."

I was stunned at his words. I'd gotten through to him. God had gotten through to him. Oh, me of little faith. Why did I ever doubt the all-powerful, all-knowing, almighty God?

I had tears in my eyes as Tyrone continued, "There was a reason behind what I did. It may not be right, and I don't want to put it on record, but given a chance, I will have my lawyer contact you. All I want to say right now is I apologize for your loss. If I could take it back, I would."

Whether he was saying this because he'd been caught or because he genuinely wished he'd never killed my son, I couldn't know. But I felt so blessed God was granting my plea that Tyrone would speak to me that I found myself smiling at him as joy washed over me like buckets of cool water on a sweltering day. Finally, I'd been promised answers as to why he'd shot my son.

Jumping up, I begged the judge. "Your Honor, would it be possible to hug him?"

My whole family and the ADA gasped. Then everything was silent except for the hammering of my heartbeat. The judge pursed her lips and stared at me. I held my breath, saying a silent prayer that God would give me this. I *really* wanted to hug Tyrone. I wanted him to feel my love.

It felt like minutes passed, though I'm sure it was only seconds. Then the judge said emphatically, "No, not for a few reasons, okay? Because he is incarcerated."

My heart dropped to the floor. Pain swept over me like a rip current grabbing hold and pulling me under. I couldn't breathe as I plummeted to the ocean's floor. Back in my seat, tears poured from my eyes like water from a faucet, knowing I wouldn't get the chance to hug Tyrone. Beside me, I could feel Mike's relief. I knew my husband well enough to guess he was figuring Tyrone might very well snap my neck if he got his large bony hands on me. But at that moment, I didn't care.

Tyrone was still staring at me, so I looked him straight in the eyes and said with complete sincerity, "I'm sending you a hug, Tyrone. I really wish I could give it to you in person."

After the sentencing, I tried to get permission to visit Tyrone in prison. I found someone willing to talk to Tyrone on my behalf, and Tyrone agreed to see me. But I wasn't able to get authorization to visit him. So I did the only thing I could. I sent him another message to let him know it wasn't my choice not to see him.

I didn't know if Tyrone had people in his life who'd let him down, but I didn't want to be one of those people. He would have a long life ahead of him in prison, and my heart broke for him. I could not explain my love for him, a love which only God could have placed in my heart. He remains on my daily prayer list, and maybe someday God will open the door for me to share God's love and forgiveness with him in person.

30. My Mistakes and Grief Process

I was codependent most of my life with both Tony and Luke. I allowed their actions to affect the way I felt.

Their happiness became the key to my joy. As a result, I became obsessed with controlling their actions and feared they would not love me if I didn't do things for them. Both Tony and Luke got upset when I took charge. Luke questioned my actions, asking why I did something for him when he was perfectly capable of doing it himself. This, in turn, destroyed some of the love Luke felt for me because it made him feel like I didn't trust him. Furthermore, when I took charge, it didn't allow Luke to grow by making his own choices and learning from his mistakes.

I learned these behaviors as a child. My parents struggled to show me love, which led me to try to find that love as an adult. Unfortunately, the cycle kept repeating itself. First with Tony, then with Luke.

When I first met Mike, I tried to control him so that he would love me too. Finally, Mike helped me work through some of my codependence issues. It took several years, but I am moving toward no longer being dependent on others now that I can clearly see how my past affected my reactions. I'm not saying I'm completely healed, but I hope someday I will be. The first step was seeing the problems that made me do what I was doing. That changed how I felt about myself. Then, to heal, I stopped trying to control other people, and it was then that I allowed myself to feel fully loved by Mike. Shortly after that, I learned to love myself. Then I felt God's love like I had never felt it before, and this changed everything.

Finally, I am happy and at peace. I trust God to care for me. Even though I knew he was always with me, most of the time I felt abandoned by him. But it wasn't God who left me—I had abandoned myself. But not anymore. The more I surrender my insecurities to God, the stronger I become.

After Luke's death, I needed to go through a similar process for my grief. These six steps—denial, anger, bargaining, depression, acceptance, and forgiveness—can help you recover from codependence and/or grief.

Denial: I kept very busy right after losing my son. Whether cleaning his room, getting ready for the funeral, attending church, or talking to friends, I always kept my mind occupied. Because if I sat still, I would have to face the fact that Luke wasn't coming home. Denial is a defense mechanism our minds use to avoid feeling overwhelmed.

Always deal with your repressed feelings because they won't go away. Feelings are energy, and when we block them, we block our energy, good and bad. This can lead to bad health, taking our anger out on our family, or causing us to miss an enjoyable moment. If you don't deal with your feelings, you won't change, and you won't grow. This is the reason you need to deal with your emotions appropriately, or they will control you. You are responsible for your feelings, and no one can tell you how to feel. Remember the old saying, "What you think influences how you feel." It is equally important to remember you are not responsible for how anyone else feels.

Anger: I became angry at myself when I realized all the times God tried to get my attention by telling me that I was putting Luke before him. If Luke needed something whenever I was supposed to attend church, I chose to help him instead of going to church. This happened in many other situations too. When God wanted me to do something, my son always came first. After his death, I believed God allowed Luke's death because I allowed Luke to replace God in my life. In turn, I partially blamed myself for Luke's death and I still do.

Everyone feels angry now and then, but you must not let it become a huge part of your life, or it will ultimately control you. Most anger is inappropriate because people haven't been taught how to deal with anger. You need to learn to deal with your anger before it becomes harmful. Sometimes your anger may make the other person angry too. Then you have a problem. This is the perfect time to surrender your anger to God and ask him to help you stop feeling angry. He will help you deal with it and make things right with the other person. It's ok to get angry when you need to, but it's not good to repress it and let it control you because your anger will eventually explode. So make sure to deal with your anger appropriately and quickly. You can even use that negative energy to complete a project you've been putting off, like cleaning your house or car. Finally, don't beat yourself up for feeling angry since it is a normal feeling that you will often experience. Think of it as a test and learn how to better deal with anger each time it happens.

Bargaining: The next thing I did was beg that if I did what God required of me, then he would take me to heaven so that I could be with my son. I thought about suicide several times, but I could never go through with it. I was concerned about how I would hurt my loved ones. Since God didn't agree to any of my negotiation tactics, I eventually gave up on bargaining.

Almost everyone has tried to bargain with God at some point in their life. I'm sure you remember a time when you've done that. We negotiate when we are desperate and can't handle our problems or when our pain becomes unbearable. Sometimes God answers our request. Other times he shows us his perspective on the situation.

Did you ever think that maybe he put you in your situation so that you would cry out to him for help? Rather than bargaining with the almighty, ask God directly for what you need. If it lines up with his will, he will grant your request.

Depression: When I realized God still had a purpose for me and that he wasn't calling me home to heaven as I begged him to, I became significantly depressed. Although I did have a few happy days, my depression went on for a long time. My husband helped pull me out of my darkness, but only after I finally let him into my world. Mike asked how I would feel if Luke could see me wallowing in my depression. Since my son didn't like anyone to feel sad, I knew he would be upset with me for not moving on and enjoying life. This was a significant turning point for me. It took time, but I am a new person living in the light again.

Acceptance: When I finally surrendered my pain and loss to God, I accepted Luke's death as part of God's plan. It was then that I forgave myself for my part in Luke's death and all of my past mistakes. God gave me peace that everything was under his complete control and that he would use my son's death for my good. It doesn't mean that I don't miss Luke. I miss him all the time as any mother that has lost a child will.

Forgiveness: After finally forgiving myself, I realized that I needed to forgive Luke for everything I held against him. So many hurts kept creeping back into my mind, and they haunted me daily. I spoke to him as if he was in the room with me. "Luke, you broke my heart numerous times with all the anguish you put me through. You asked me to do so many terrible things for you that no other parent would've done for their child. Yet, I loved you so much, and since I didn't know how to show you that love, I did everything you asked of me, even though I knew it was wrong. I forgive you for the hurt you caused. I forgive you for the many days when I got up in the morning and prayed, 'God, just let me get through the day without something going wrong. Please, just give me one day of peace. One day without Luke getting arrested or taking his anger out on me. One day Mike and I don't worry about Luke hurting one of us, whether physically or mentally. Please, Lord, I beg you. Amen.' I love you, son, and I will see you when we are reunited in heaven." A tidal wave of relief washed over me after I forgave Luke and allowed God to heal me.

Anyone who has experienced loss will go through these steps. If you don't, you will self-destruct. It is a process. The steps may present themselves in a different order, or some steps may pass relatively quickly, whereas others may last for years. I struggled with depression for a long time. Even now, I still have bad days.

Just remember that acceptance is the first step to surrendering your pain. When you admit that you are powerless, you can move forward. Next, find someone to talk to or a group to join. Most important, talk honestly to God, who loves each of us more than we will ever know. Don't be afraid to tell him your fears, concerns, and anger issues because he already knows them. Surrender all your pain to him and see yourself for who you really are. We are created in God's image, and we are all valuable to him. Admit your deepest, darkest feelings to him. Share them with a trusted friend too. This will help with the healing, especially if the friend has been through a similar circumstance.

Next, humbly ask God to mold you by admitting your mistakes and failures and allow him to comfort you with his peace. You need to acknowledge to God that you hurt yourself by your choice of actions and accept the forgiveness he gives to all believers. Finally, forgive yourself, just like God forgave you. Pray daily and ask God to speak to you by reading your Bible. Fill your mind by memorizing verses. Ask God for direction and follow where he leads through his power and strength by allowing him to care for you. This will help you to love yourself like you never have before.

When you feel God changing you, you will start to feel better. You will heal, and a sense of peace will surround you every day.

31. ASSURANCE

January 24, 2019, would have been Luke's twenty-first birthday. That day, I received a call from the Johnstown Police Department saying that I could pick up the necklace he'd been wearing the night of his murder. It was as though I was receiving a gift for Luke's birthday.

The necklace was one of two matching gold cross pendants Tony had purchased for me for Christmas when I was eighteen. I'd given Tony's necklace to Luke when he reached his teens, and it was among his most prized possessions. He never took it off. The necklace had still been around his neck when the police arrived on the scene. But though Luke was lying in a pool of his own blood, not one drop had touched the cross.

To me, that was a miracle, a sign sent from God that he was in control and held Luke in his loving arms. After I picked up the necklace from the police station, I drove to the place where Luke had taken his last breath. Standing in the exact spot where he'd died, I slipped the necklace that had once been Tony's around my neck. As it entwined with my own, I felt Luke's presence with me.

My heart still breaks from the daily emptiness I feel from my loss. I know I will see my son again in heaven, but I will continue to grieve his death until then.

In October, I received a collect call from the prison asking if I'd accept charges from Tyrone. I did so gladly. He'd never followed through with having his lawyer communicate as to the circumstances of shooting Luke. So maybe I was finally about to find out.

But when "Tyrone" started talking, he didn't know who I was and claimed to be trying to reach someone in Alabama. I realized this wasn't my son's killer but a different Tyrone. I was deeply disappointed as I'd thought God was answering my prayers to speak with Tyrone. Still, nothing is impossible for our all-powerful God, so I am continuing to wait patiently for God's timing when maybe I can share face-to-face with Tyrone how much God loves him.

Luke came to visit me in another dream. This time Mike and Jessica were both with me in the dream. I asked Luke if he knew he was dead. He thought about it and said, "No." So I told him he'd been shot and killed.

"It's all good," he responded, not seeming upset at all.

Then I told him his cat Kayley had passed away too. At that moment, she appeared on Mike's lap. She was purring and rolling around. Both my son and his cat seemed completely at peace. We had an enjoyable conversation, and he mentioned his biological dad Tony, though I don't remember the specifics.

Although waking up from such dreams are painful, I love spending some time with my son. Even if I have to accept that Luke is no longer on this earth, I can allow myself to be with him through my memories, and this allows me to heal. If I try to escape the pain by choosing not to remember him, then I deprive myself of every memory of my son, from his first breath to his last heartbeat. So I choose the pain so I can keep Luke with me until we meet again.

Despite the dreams and comfort God sent me, I still struggled with doubts about whether Luke was in heaven. I longed for some absolute assurance that my son had faith in Jesus Christ when he passed away and would be with me in eternity. After my mother-in-law's funeral, Luke had told me he didn't believe in God. But I sensed he was just angry and trying to hurt me for making him go to rehab. I reminded him of how he accepted Jesus Christ as his Savior at the age of seven.

Still, that nagging concern continued to plague me. Then a few months after the sentencing, the friend my son had been staying with when he was murdered finally agreed to talk to me again. To my surprise, he brought up the subject of faith entirely of his own accord. He told me that Luke had spoken to him numerous times about God, urging him to place his faith in Christ. I knew he wasn't making this up, because he used the exact words I had used when I told Luke about Jesus. What a blessing it was to know that even in those difficult last months when he was struggling with so many mental and emotional issues, Luke had witnessed to his friend about God and told him to let Jesus into his life.

For me, it was also a priceless gift. The greatest anyone has ever given me on this earth. Knowing Luke cared enough to worry about his own salvation and the salvation of those around him gave me the absolute certainty that Luke's faith in Jesus Christ was genuine. From that moment, such a weight was lifted off me. I now have absolute peace that my son is waiting for me in heaven, and I will see him again one day.

·♥·♥·♥·♥·♥·

God opened the door to prompt Luke's friend to give me this gift of peace and reassurance. If you've never received Jesus Christ as Savior, God is knocking on the door of your heart to offer you the same gift of forgiveness and eternal life in Jesus Christ that he gave my son. The same gift that God offers my son's killer.

If you haven't accepted Jesus as your Lord and Savior, will you do it now before it's too late? If so, just pray in your heart the prayer I prayed all those years ago with Luke, which you will find below, or use your own words.

A SINNER'S PRAYER: Dear Jesus, I believe in you. I believe you are the Son of God, that you died for my sins, and that you were buried and rose again as written in the Bible. Please come into my heart so I can have eternal life. Thank you for giving me the Holy Spirit to help me live the way you want me to live. Forgive me for my past sins. Guide me in my future so that I can live my life for you. Amen.

If you've prayed the sinner's prayer, welcome to God's family.

32. I Love You!

Imagine if my son hadn't called me before he died with the parting words, "I love you." My final memory of him would be very different. Having "I love you" as the last words said by someone who has passed on is a memory to treasure forever.

It's equally important to regularly tell our friends and family that we love them. What if you never see that person again? I didn't know I'd never speak to my son again when we exchanged that final casual conversation. Tell everyone what you want to say to them *now* because you never know how much your words may mean later.

For much of my life, I had no memory of my dad ever saying those most important three little profound words every person wants to hear. Because of this, I felt unworthy of love, which in turn led me down a lot of dark paths. While at my son's funeral, I walked over to my dad and mustered up the courage to tell him how I felt.

"You know, Dad, I have never once heard you tell me that you love me. It really hurts not to hear those words from you. I hope that you can someday tell me before it's too late. I love you, Dad, and I forgive you for all the times that you've hurt me."

He made no reply. Sadly, tears clouding my vision, I walked away. Three days later, I was out in my driveway when my dad pulled in. He said a few inconsequential things. Then he got back in his truck. He started the engine, but instead of pulling out, he looked right at me and said, "I love you."

Then he quickly backed out of the driveway and drove off. I almost fell to the ground in shock, my heart pumping hard and my knees turning to jelly. After forty-six years, I'd finally heard the most precious three words anyone can say. That was the best gift my dad has ever given me. I will never forget that moment.

My sister phoned me a few weeks later to say Dad had called to tell her he loved her. He also started telling Mom, "I love you." Those three simple, short words changed all of our lives. Our relationships improved, and we connected on a deeper level.

Dad, Mike, and I joined a weekly pool league. I finally had the father my girlfriends had. The father I dreamed of having all of my life. Of course, I was upset when spring came and the league ended. But then, we joined a monthly cornhole tournament. I can't wait to see what the future holds for our renewed family.

The following year after Luke went home to be with the Lord, I sensed God calling me to tell the world my story. Writing this book meant reliving all the trauma. Then I had to relive it again and again each time I edited the manuscript. Going through all my videos pushed me close to giving up on life.

But I knew God had called me to do this and that this was for his glory. God has given me the message to tell each and every person I come across that he loves them. I can only pray my story will touch many lives and help others who have been in similar situations.

My early life was full of disobedience. I am genuinely sorry for all the mistakes I have made. And there are many. I put myself in positions where I was tempted. As a result, I've had to learn the hard way. But God is a God of love and forgiveness, and I know he has forgiven me for my many mistakes. I'm so glad God isn't finished with me yet. He is lighting my path and leading me out of the darkness into his marvelous light (1 Peter 2:9).

I understand now that if there weren't any valleys, any hard times, there would be no way for us to grow to become our best selves and acquire the faith God wants us to have. I've never felt so strong and courageous as I have since losing my son. My faith became bottomless. I never doubted God's plan through all of my pain. The well-known theologian, pastor, and Christian author Charles Stanley once said:

"Every person is born with a deep desire to be loved unconditionally, but when this yearning is not fully met, many hurts and scars can result. What security and wholeness there is in knowing that we can call God "our Father" and receive that unconditional love!"

I am thankful God has blessed me with my wonderful husband Mike, through whom God has shown me his unconditional love. Mike has stuck by me through all my ups and downs. He is my rock and the most amazing person I've ever met. When it seems I can't go on, Mike reminds me I have a story to tell, and there are people who need to feel God's love through me. That work will continue until God decides it is time to call me home, as the apostle Paul describes:

"Being confident of this, that he who began a good work in you will carry it on to completion until the day of Christ Jesus." (Phil. 1:6)

What hardship or valley is God taking you through right now? He is there to help you through it. Are you struggling with loss? Is there someone you need to love or forgive? Maybe you need to love or forgive yourself. If you want peace, you *must* forgive. It's not an option. I know it's hard to forgive, but keep trying. Don't ever give up.

Whatever your problem, God is the answer. I know he is because he is the one who has helped me every step of the way. He is all-powerful and all-knowing. He knows what we need and how to help us before we even know we need help (Matt. 6:8). God can show you his forgiveness too. He can give you faith such as he's given me. When all hope seems lost, he is our only hope.

One thing we must always keep in mind is that physical death is not the end. Where we spend our eternity is what is most important. We are all born with sinful, selfish hearts, as God's Word states clearly:

"The heart is deceitful above all things and beyond cure. Who can understand it?" (Jer. 17:9)

I followed my own deceitful, sinful heart when I chose Tony over God. Only when I received God's forgiveness in faith was my life transformed and set on a new path. You only have one life and one chance to accept God's free gift of everlasting life through grace.

Today despite my painful past and loss of my son, I am blessed. My relationship with my mom has been restored and is better than it has ever been. Every year, I celebrate Luke's earthly birthday and heavenly birthday with some of his friends, who I'm proud to consider my own children. My heart and my life are full of love.

On Christmas Day, 2020, I sent a letter to Tyrone, my son's killer. In the letter, I reminded him that I have forgiven him. "May the peace of my God cover you in his grace. May you feel his love for you. I am sending my love too." I asked again if he'd let me visit him. I want to show Tyrone my love, and by doing so, help Tyrone see God's love.

God wants me to show his love to everyone. That is the reason I am writing this book. Will you accept God's love? I can't wait until the day comes when I am reunited with my son and meet Jesus face-to-face. Until then, I will continue to love the unlovable and to forgive as I have been forgiven.

·♥·♥·♥·♥·♥·

Want to follow Tammy as she travels the world, finding adventure one journey at a time, even if it involves meeting a killer in court or prison, visiting national parks, or seeing gorgeous beaches? Click or type https://mybook.to/TammyHorvath into your internet search bar to read Book 2 or see all books in the Journeys Through Life memoir series.

Life Begins with Travel: Facing My Fears. Finding My Smile.

A husband dead in a fiery crash. A son claimed by a killer's hand. Tammy Horvath doesn't think she'll ever smile again.

Strengthened by her faith, she bravely heads solo to Iceland to see the northern lights, where she climbs glaciers and ventures into caves before seizing the opportunity to travel more often.

Tammy will take you on a journey of love, laughter, and inspirational life lessons as she swims in the crystal-clear Caribbean Sea, gets stuck atop one of Mexico's pyramids, endures a tropical storm in the Bahamas, and hikes amid Yellowstone National Park's spectacular scenery.

Will life's tragedies make Tammy cower in fear forever? Or can she embrace a world of adventure and find happiness again?

· ♥ · ♥ · ♥ · ♥ · ♥ ·

If you enjoyed *Gone in an Instant,* please consider leaving a review to help other readers find a book they will love. You can submit a review wherever you find my book, even if you didn't buy it there. Just a few words will make a huge difference.

Just click or type the link below into your internet search bar.

Amazon review link: https://www.amazon.com/review/create-review?asin=B09PJQWNYV

Goodreads review link: https://www.goodreads.com/book/show/60184390-gone-in-an-instant

In Case You Missed It—Also by Tammy Horvath

Gone in an Instant: Losing My Son. Loving His Killer. **Book 1**

A son killed by a single bullet. A mother's heart shattered. As Tammy Horvath struggles to come to terms with her son's death, a voice tells her to forgive his killer.

With her soul tormented by the loss of her son, Tammy fights to get out of bed every day because she can't face a seemingly hopeless future. But Luke would want her to be happy. So she pushes forward and embarks on a journey, searching for peace, hope, and a chance to keep her son alive in her heart.

Will God reveal himself and set her free in a way she could never have imagined? Or will Tammy's spirit remain broken by one man's deed?

Life Begins with Travel: Facing My Fears. Finding My Smile. **Book 2**

A husband dead in a fiery crash. A son claimed by a killer's hand. Tammy Horvath doesn't think she'll ever smile again.

Strengthened by her faith, she bravely heads solo to Iceland to see the northern lights, where she climbs glaciers and ventures into caves before seizing the opportunity to travel more often.

Tammy will take you on a journey of love, laughter, and inspirational life lessons as she swims in the crystal-clear Caribbean Sea, gets stuck atop one of

Mexico's pyramids, endures a tropical storm in the Bahamas, and hikes amid Yellowstone National Park's spectacular scenery.

Will life's tragedies make Tammy cower in fear forever? Or can she embrace a world of adventure and find happiness again?

Deep Inside: Forgiving the Unforgivable. Loving the Unlovable. Book 3

A chilling behind-bars encounter with a killer unfolds. Step into the heart-wrenching world of his victim's grieving mother. Can the unforgivable be forgiven?

As Tammy Horvath grapples with the weight of depression following her profound loss, she discovers that no amount of exercise can completely mend her shattered soul. The quest for genuine healing takes a courageous turn as she confronts the murderer, unraveling the haunting mysteries behind Luke's tragic death.

Are the roots of Tammy's faith deep enough to make a difference? Or are Tammy's friends right in warning her against facing a cold-blooded killer?

Exploring Mountains and Beaches: Journeys Beyond Borders. Adventures Worth Pursuing. Book 4

What do you hold dear in life? For Tammy Horvath, it's the relentless pursuit of connecting with others, exploring new horizons alive with wonder, and seizing every moment while she checks off items on her bucket list.

As Tammy explores mountains and beaches in paradise, she's fueled by the allure of new cultures, creating memories that have made her who she is today. Throughout her island adventures to the Bahamas, Turks and Caicos, and Curacao, as well as hikes through national parks in the Canadian Rocky Mountains, surprises lurk at every turn—from navigating floods to fending off avian ambushes. Embracing the chaos, Tammy turns each misadventure into a story worth telling.

Join Tammy on this journey beyond borders, where each step brings her closer to the beauty of life.

One Text Away: A Doctor's Indecent Proposal. **Book 5**

In this true story, Tammy Horvath faces an indecent proposal from a respected younger doctor while she grapples with an unrelated daunting health scare: a breast lump that grows larger, demanding immediate action. Tammy must confront her deepest fears and let faith be her compass, forgiveness her guide, and self-discovery her destination.

Will the doctor's enticing compliments threaten Tammy's resolve to remain a faithful wife, causing her to destroy her marriage? Or will she have enough self-control to resist Adonis's charm?

Click or type https://mybook.to/TammyHorvath into your internet search bar, then choose a book to purchase an eBook, paperback, or audiobook of any book in the series recorded by Tammy Horvath. All books are available on Kindle Unlimited.

NOTE TO THE READER

About the Author

Author and speaker Tammy Horvath was born and raised on a floodplain in western Pennsylvania, where she currently resides with her amazing husband Michael. She has three wonderful adult stepchildren, along with her only child Luke, who is now in heaven with his Creator and finally at peace.

Tammy has almost three decades of administrative experience in real estate and insurance. She has volunteered for more than a decade with a Christian nonprofit providing education and other essential needs for at-risk children around the world. She has been a spokesperson for the nonprofit's needs, served in church ministries, and is always available to share her story and God's message of love and forgiveness.

Tammy and her husband still live in the same house where they raised Luke, even though she cries every time she enters his room.

Tammy will never stop grieving the loss of her only son Luke to a murderer's bullet. But she lives and writes with the assurance that she will see him again and that God will ultimately use her son's death for good. She loves sharing treasured memories of her son with anyone who will listen.

Tammy has written five books in the Journeys Through Life memoir series:

Remember that one person who hurt you, the one you can't forgive? In her first book, ***Gone in an Instant***, Tammy tells the heartbreaking story of losing her son to a murderer's bullet and the road she traveled to forgive his killer. Being vulnerable about her past and her mistakes helps readers start to explore their own. The last few chapters reveal a pathway to overcome failures and find freedom, just like Tammy did. It took time, but recently, she's been visiting Tyrone in prison. As a perfectionist, Tammy refuses to give up on anyone—even a murderer.

How do you attempt to escape what has caused you the most pain? Despite thump-in-the-stomach-harrowing challenges, Tammy's second book, ***Life Begins with Travel***, reveals how embarking on a courageous journey to new destinations can cultivate emotional healing. Travel became the coping mechanism that she needed. Conquering her fears as she shares the smells, the tastes, the bumps and bruises acquired on her travels changed her and helped keep Tammy from getting stuck on the top of pyramids as she did in Mexico. The one irreconcilable truth from these stories is that travel is always transformational.

How do you navigate the suffocating weight of depression that follows a life-changing loss? A coroner's knock on Tammy's door changes her life forever. In her third book, ***Deep Inside***, she tries to escape the pain through exercise. But to experience genuine healing, she must summon the courage to face the man who murdered Luke to unravel the haunting mysteries behind her son's tragic death. But only if she can pass the prison's high-tech security protocols. Are Tammy's friends right in warning her against facing a cold-blooded killer?

Do you have a bucket list that involves travel? Tammy loves to seize the moment and live life to the full by immersing herself in new cultures, feeling the warm sand between her toes on stunning beaches, and marveling at the grandeur of the Canadian Rockies' majestic mountains. Join Tammy on this thrilling journey where chaos awaits, and each misadventure unfolds into unforgettable tales in her fourth book, ***Exploring Mountains and Beaches***.

Have you ever been tempted to have an affair? When a breast lump grows exponentially in one year, the doctor demands a biopsy. While dealing with stress, Tammy wrestles with the demons of insecurity when a handsome young doctor tries to sweep her off her feet. Like an addicted gambler, she considers putting it all in and betting on the win to satisfy her lust. Prepare to be captivated as Tammy navigates the shadows of doubt, trying to emerge into the light of hope in *One Text Away*, book five in the Journeys Through Life series.

Ultimately, Tammy writes and speaks so that every reader may know God's immeasurable love and that forgiveness is the essence of God's love. She can't wait for the day she meets God face-to-face and is reunited with her son and other loved ones in heaven.

Click or type https://mybook.to/TammyHorvath into your internet search bar, then choose a book to purchase an eBook, paperback, or audiobook of any book in the series recorded by Tammy Horvath. All books are available on Kindle Unlimited.

Chat with the author and other memoir authors and readers by joining the friendly, fun Facebook group We Love Memoirs at https://www.facebook.com/groups/welovememoirs/.

Made in the USA
Las Vegas, NV
27 March 2025

20173027R00100